NOTES FOR

A GLOSSARY OF WORDS

AND PHRASES

OF

BARBADIAN DIALECT

FRANK A. COLLYMORE

Acknowledgements

The sixth edition of this volume, with a more modern typeface, a new cover and a Foreword by Edward Baugh, has been made possible by generous donations from:

BANKS (BARBADOS) BREWERIES LTD.

and

SHELL ANTILLES AND GUIANAS LTD.

The Barbados National Trust extends our appreciation for the continuing support of these corporate sponsors.

July 1992

Front Cover photographs by Ronnie Carrington

For Ellice

First Published 1955
Second Impression 1956
Second Edition 1957
Third Edition 1965
Fourth Edition 1970
The Barbados National Trust
Fifth Edition 1976
Sixth Edition 1992

PREFACE TO THE FIRST EDITION

These notes together with the Introduction were first published in *Bim* (Vols. 5 & 6, Nos. 17-22), and now owe their appearance in book form to the requests of several readers.

I should like to thank all those who have assisted in this compilation, especially Mrs. H. H. Bayley, Messrs. Eustace M. Shilstone, Aubrey Douglas-Smith, Fred Kirton, and W. Therold Barnes, Dr. A. J. Clarke, and the Staff of Combermere School.

I must again emphasize the fact, mentioned in the Introduction, that the notes make no pretension to anything but an amateur approach to the subject.

PREFACE TO THE SECOND EDITION

Some hundred and fifty new words and phrases have been included in this edition, and a few of those, published in the first edition, which proved on closer scrutiny not to have been exclusively Barbadian in origin and use have been discarded.

I should like to thank all those who have assisted me: in addition to those already mentioned I should like to add the names of Miss A. Packer, Dr. John B. Lewis, Dr. Kevin Earle, Messrs. Basil Ward, E. M. McConney, Kirk Shiwell, Errol Hill, Neville Connell, Frank Gibbons and especially Miss Margot Blackman who supplied many of the words and phrases from the Windward parishes.

PREFACE TO THE THIRD EDITION

My thanks are due to the Tourist Board without whose generous assistance this third edition would not have been possible.

About ninety additional words and phrases have been included.

PREFACE TO THE FOURTH EDITION

My thanks are again due to the Tourist Board for their generous assistance towards the publication of this new edition.

About two dozen additional words and phrases have been included.

F.A.C.

PREFACE TO THE FIFTH EDITION

The initiative of the Barbados National Trust in undertaking the publication of this fifth edition is most gratefully appreciated. The encouraging demand for the Notes indicates a widening interest among Barbadians and Barbadophiles and this new edition offers a welcome opportunity to add a number of words and phrases which have come to attention since the fourth edition came out. It must be stressed once more that the collection is not to be regarded as a work of scholarship or erudition but simply the expression of an amateur's interest in the richness of the Barbadian vocabulary.

John Wickham

FOREWORD

If we judge by the number of reprintings which it has had, and by the continuing demand for it, *Barbadian Dialect* is Frank Collymore's most successful book, and in a sense his most useful. Success or not, it is certainly a little treasure trove of Bajan heritage. Its usefulness, whether to scholar or layman, to visitor or native is accompanied by pleasure, a pleasure which derives ultimately from the delight which the compiler himself obviously took in the collecting of material and in the formulating of definitions, explanations and comments. The sense of fun, sometimes wry, is communicated, for example, when, having glossed **meat** as "cane-**meat** or fodder," he adds, "A statement like *I just gave the horse the meat* is likely to prove disconcerting unless the local use of the word is borne in mind."

The glossary's unpretentious and admittedly, winsomely amateur character (and it is important to remember that he sensibly called it *Notes for a Glossary*) is an important factor of its appeal. It is the sort of book that one dips into just to see what delicious tit-bit one might find, and not just when one needs to look up a particular word or phrase. At the same time, it has provided an inviting foundation on which persons of like mind, as well as more complete scholars can build. One hopes, though, that no dictates of strict scholarship will ever deprive us of those genial and personal touches, however gratuitous, which help to give *Barbadian Dialect* its special quality; as when, for instance, Collymore leads into the definition of **bag-blind** by explaining his initial wrong conjecture as to its meaning.

The personality and dynamic which we sense in even so factual a thing as this glossary is of a piece with all other aspects of Collymore's work, and an integral part of that deep, yet never solemn feeling for his native place and its people. It is a feeling which informed his long and memorable career as a schoolteacher, which informed his poetry, his short stories, his "voicing" of the dialect whether in his brilliant radio readings of Bajan short stories or in his legendary stage performances. It informed too his great pioneering work with the little magazine *Bim*, mention of which reminds us to set the glossary in the wider context of his contribution to the conservation and nurturing of West Indian cultural heritage.

It is all one - whether he is giving the meaning of the "charmingly ironic euphemism" **rose tree trimmer**, or describing in verse the ostensibly commonplace and inconsequential blue agave which clings to "the barren (windswept) hillside":

> Armoured against forgotten fate
> They score the low horizon, fronting
> The long deliberate curve of the bay;
> Holding within their pale blue depths
> Their guarded secret, their untamed beauty.

In the agave, Collymore finds a symbol for the resilience of place and people, including, perhaps especially the most lowly placed, like the old woman seen at "Day's End" at the "neglected fringe of a fishing-village," who, though "shrivelled with age," walked "with stark unconscious pride".

A people's language is the distillation of their culture. That celebrated or notorious "Englishness" of the Bajan character cannot be understood without some understanding of what they have done with English. Collymore understood, intimately and with love.

Edward Baugh
Department of English
University of the West Indies,
Mona, Jamaica.

17 July, 1992

INTRODUCTION

Some months ago I began, in an amateurish sort of way, making a collection of words and phrases in use in our local dialect with the idea of compiling a glossary. I very soon became aware that the accomplishment of this purpose demanded far more time and research than were at my disposal, a far wider knowledge of the historical background of the island than I possess — in a word, far more than the amateur approach. And yet, at the same time I did not wish to abandon my plan altogether, for I believed that the notes I had made might prove interesting, and might act as a stimulus to others more qualified for the task. Consequently I decided, not without trepidation, to publish the notes. A similar series of notes was published some twenty-odd years ago in *The Harrisonian.* I do not know whether any others exist.

A Barbadian who tries to compile such a series labours under a handicap at the outset: he cannot always be quite certain what words are *Standard English and what are not. Take gap, scotch, and tot, for example. He is worried when first he consults a dictionary to discover that a gap is not an entrance or driveway to a residence, that digging one's heels in the earth in order to secure a foothold is not scotching, and that a tot is not a drinking-vessel made of tin. These words have carried these meanings for him all his life; his confidence is shaken. In these notes, therefore, there must be omissions due to this cause.

The authorities on Standard English in the compilation of these notes have been (a) the Concise Oxford Dictionary (referred to hereinafter as the C.O.D.) as regards modern English usage of words and phrases, and (b) the Shorter Oxford English Dictionary (S.O.E.D. in the notes), in tracing such words as have become obsolete in modern Standard English.

---

* "When we speak of Good English, or Standard English, or Pure English, as distinct from ... Provincial English (the dialects proper), we must remember that there is nothing in the original nature of these other dialects which is in itself inferior, or reprehensible, or contemptible. In a word, the other dialects are in reality, and apart from fashion and custom, quite as good as Standard English, considered simply as forms of language; but they have not the same place in general estimation, they have not been so highly cultivated ... and they have not the same wide currency."

Professor H.C.K. Wyld: *The Growth of English*

It must not be inferred, of course, that Barbadian is one of the "dialects proper"; yet,. shorn of its illiteracies, it might well claim consideration as such.

I have not attempted to list all the local names of our flora and fauna; only those that for some reason or other, such as by their quaintness or their aptness, seemed noteworthy.

The origins and derivations of many words present another problem; but this is the province of the etymologist, and I have been able to do little more than throw out, here and there, a suggestion.

Mr. Eric Partridge writes in his *World of Words* "A dialect is that variety of language which prevails in a district and has local peculiarities of vocabulary, pronunciation, and phrase." Again, with reference to pronunciation, our dialect presents such intricacies of accent, intonation, and phonetics, that it would be quite impossible for me to do more than try to indicate, when occasion arises, the sound of some unusual word.

When all these points are borne in mind, it is to be hoped that the words "not without trepidation" will be appreciated, and that these notes will be regarded in their true perspective.

Many words in this collection will be discovered upon closer scrutiny to be survivals in modern Standard English, either obsolete, like *cock-loft, kill-cow,* and *token* (omen), or archaisms, like peradventure, *nigh* (adverb), and *renege*: or else, like *mould* (of the head), *lambaste,* and *ca(r)fuffle* in use in various English dialects today; some, such as *boar-cat, holler* and *god horse,* current in the U.S.; a great many — *fortyleg, forced-ripe, merrywing, nimbles, pompasett* for example, — the coinage of local wit and invention.

Barbados has always been British; and it is to be expected therefore that there are few words in our dialect of foreign origin: what is remarkable, however, is the fact that there seem to be so very few words of African derivation.

Many of the examples quoted will be observed to be ungrammatical: I thought it best that the raciness of the dialect might often be best presented in the raw.

It must also be borne in mind that many of the words and phrases are not peculiar to Barbados: It would be interesting to discover how many of them are in common circulation elsewhere in the Caribbean, and, for that matter, the Southern States of the U.S.A.

In conclusion, I should like to thank those who have assisted in bringing words and phrases to my notice; and to state that any additions to, or, corrections and criticism of, the notes will be welcomed.

NOTES FOR

A GLOSSARY OF WORDS AND PHRASES

OF

BARBADIAN DIALECT

A.

able. Able for, fit to cope with. *Arthur too bad — I ain't able with him.* J. Graham Cruikshank: *Black Talk.*

above. If you were told that Mr. X was *above the house*, you wouldn't expect to observe him hovering over the roof; you would look for him somewhere to the windward (east) side of the building. **Above** and **below** are frequently used in this sense; but these rough and ready definitions cannot be regarded as comprehensive. Indeed their use, together with those of **upperside** and **low(er) side, up** and **down**, is often so confusing to the enquiring visitor that, "Barbadians must have an almost automatic and instinctive awareness of the points of the compass not vouchsafed to **foreigners.**"

acid. (Slang) Rum. See **fire** the acid.

across. A correspondent writes: "This, like all Barbadian words of direction, is used so instinctively by Barbadians that almost all of them are astonished, and incredulous that they are practically unintelligible to all but the native-born. An Englishman told to *go across* looks for a road or river to cross, and probably does cross the road; the Barbadian probably wants him to go along the road..." I should say, as a Barbadian, that *across* means any direction taken along a road which crosses the first road indicated, or which turns away from it at a sufficiently sharp angle.

admirals. The name of the locally made biscuit (six for a cent, I believe), popular during the first decade of this century.

admire. Still occasionally used in its original sense of "view with wonder or surprise; to marvel at. 1590" S.O.E.D…as, *'Long the St. Philip coast you does have to admire the wind.*

after. In telling the time a quarter after is frequently used instead of the Standard English "past".

afternoon. A euphemism for backside.

again. Often used colloquially in the sense of now, at this particular moment. *I'm not going to town again* would imply that the speaker had changed his mind, he had decided not to go now.

akee. There are few specimens of the true akee tree in Barbados; what are known as akees are the fruit of the guinep tree. The roundish green berries containing a large seed surrounded by sweetish pulp are sold by the bunch, and are especially attractive to the youthful palate.

all. The following idomatic uses of this word may be noted: (1) all **about**: everywhere, as, *He went all about spreading the news:* (ii) all a **penny**: before the advent of the refrigerator an extra large catch of flying fish would result in their being sold *all a penny,* i.e., a purchaser might buy as many fish as he could conveniently need for a penny; (iii) all **is one**: it's all one, it's all the same: (iv) all **two,** and indeed, **all two both,** need no explanation; (v) all **you,** or **you all**: all of you; frequently used in addressing two persons only; (vi) **at** all is sometimes used in the sense of whatever, as, *But what it is at all you saying?* (vii) implying the idea of also, too; as, *You and all want beating.*

Allambys, The. *In the hands of the Allambys* is a current phrase which signifies to be in dire straits without chance of a reprieve. The Allambys were a family of money lenders and debt collectors who flourished in the early years of the nineteenth century, and whose methods of exacting payment were ruthless, effective, and at times, to say the least, highly original. For example, should some unfortunate prove negligent in repaying his loan, they would remind him of his shortcoming at the most inopportune moments: their favourite mode of approach being to wait until the gentleman in

2

question, in the company of his friends and acquaintances, was leaving church after divine service, when one of the Allambys would accost him in a loud whisper: "What about that little amount you promised to pay us last week, eh?"

all's right for all right is very common.

alpargatas. Leather-soled slippers with canvas straps as uppers.

animal-flower. (listed in the S.O.E.D.) The sea anemone. The Animal-Flower Cave in the parish of St. Lucy is one of the places of interest mentioned in the guide books. Apparently the name was conferred upon the sea anemone by the Rev. Griffith Hughes in his *The Natural History of Barbados* (1750). In an article, *Griffith Hughes Dissected* by Francis James Dallet *(Journal of the B.M.H.S., Vol. XXIII, No.1),* the author after quoting extracts from a critical review of the period which states that Hughes "gives not a single generical name but only English names" and "the very worst English of West-India planters", cites as an example: "In the ninth book he rather pathetically feels he had discovered a new class of beings, 'under the name of Animal Flowers'".

arrow. The cane-arrow, the flower of the sugar cane. The long slim stalks with their pearl-grey, feathery plumes could hardly have been named otherwise. Canes are said to be *in arrow*: cf. the term *en fleche* (French West Indies). The S.O.E.D. lists the word as "the leading shoot of plant or tree. 1580. To shoot into blossom as the sugar cane."

article. Polite appellation for the chamber-pot.

artificials. (Rare) Sometimes used to mean objects, especially when the name of the articles in question has escaped the memory of the speaker: *Boy, hand me a couple of those artificials there.*

as. With stress laid on this word, it is the equivalent of "as soon as". *As I hear, I'll let you know.*

asked out. invited out. Also used facetiously, as, *I see you're asked out,* which would imply that the trousers of the boy addressed were torn in the seat. When it is borne in mind that the final consonant in *ask*, as in so many other words, is not pronounced, or at best, slurred, the pun is obvious.

assified. Asinine, stupid. Not listed in C.O.D., but S.O.E.D. contains "assify" (1804).

aunt. The term aunt is rarely employed directly. A woman will not say that such and such a child is her niece, but *She* (the child) *is to call me aunt*: similarly the child will say when referring to her aunt, *I am to call her aunt*. The relationship of the aunt appears to be an ambivalent one: frequently referred to as dear-aunt, she would seem to be the most favoured relative; but when it is remembered that the expression *to be living at one's aunt* is synonymous with "living in hell", it is obvious that there is a sinister aspect to the relationship.

auntie-man. (Rare). A fussy, effeminate man. Perhaps better expressed by the patois synonym *mamapoule*.

away. Abroad, overseas; as *He comes from away,* or, *I bought this away*.

ax. As in many other dialects, is preferred to *ask*.

B.

baby. Two sixteenth century uses of this word are still common: (i) a doll, although the term **doll-baby** is more usual; (ii) the pupil of the eye: *He got struck in the baby of his eye.* Properly speaking, the baby is "the small image of oneself reflected in another's eyes" (S.O.E.D.) Cf. "You blame me too, because I can't devise Some sport to please those Babies in your eyes." Herrick: *Hesperides*.

back. (Adverb). Most often used with the meaning, again; as *This can use back.* (This can be used again); sometimes redundantly, as *I went back in* (I went in), or *I went back upstairs* (I went upstairs); and at other times with the idea of restoration, as, *This can mend back* (This can be mended), or *I shall ask him back for* *the book* (I shall ask him to return the book to me). (Verb). To turn one's back on someone, or, to have one's back towards someone or something, as *It's not polite to back anyone. I was backing the door when he came in, so I didn't see him.*

back-back. To go back, or to cause to go back. *Man, why you don't back-back the horse?*

back-biter. In the catching of crabs, the **crabber** seizes his victim from the rear, placing his fingers across its back, and is thus out of reach of the waving claws. The back-biter, however, has developed a technique of manipulating its claws in such a way that the crabber has to be especially wary in order to avoid being nipped.

backra, buckra. The C.O.D. reads "adj. and noun. (negro dialect). Characteristic of, belonging to, the white man; (noun) white man, master, (etymology doubtful: perhaps from Surinam Negro patois *bakra master*)". Only the form *backra* is used locally, and then usually contemptuously, *poor backra, backra johnny*: it is never used to mean *master.*

backyard. Any piece of enclosed land aback of a house. Not listed in C.O.D., but in current use in U.S. Backyard **cricket,** an improvised game of cricket played by a few boys in such surroundings.

bad. Bad-bowels: applied to any disorder of the bowels; bad-**feels**: "...elastic enough to include such divergent complaints as high blood-pressure, diabetes, pulmonary tuberculosis or peptic ulcer — any disease in fact where general malaise is a prominent feature". Iris Bayley: *The Bush-teas of Barbados, The Journal of the Barbados Museum and Historical Society, Vol. XVI, No.3.*: bad-**flesh**: unhealthy tissue or affected skin immediately surrounding sore, ulcer, etc.; bad-**lucky**: unlucky; bad-**minded**: evil-minded; bad-**nasty**: (with reference to health) as, a bad-nasty cold, cut etc.; the bad-**sick**: venereal disease. To **play bad**: to be aggressive or rude. Used of children, or, mockingly, of grown-ups. Bad-**play**. This expression must not be confused with **play bad**, to act in a rough boisterous manner. To bad-play is not 'to play the game', in other words to be deceitful, even unfaithful, as, *Everybody knows she bad-playing she boy friend.* The adjective is frequently used as

5

an adverb of degree to signify 'very much' or 'more than I can express', as may be gathered from the words of a popular song 'You Sweeten Me':

> *Darlin' I love you bad, so very bad, so very bad*
> *You have me goin' so mad, you sweeten me, girl, you sweeten me.*

bag-blind. When first I heard this compound used — 'a bag-blind bastard' — it called to mind Lancelot Gobbo's 'sand-blind' and 'high gravel blind' from *The Merchant of Venice* and I wondered if there might be some affinity between them; but no, the epithet was definitely not an Elizabethan relic. I was to learn later that people in very poor circumstances often use crocus bags as window curtains or blinds: hence the term would indicate that the person addressed came from a very humble home.

bag-fuzz. Loose fibres obtained from **crocus bag**. *He collecting bag-fuzz to make cord for the kite flying.*

bake. (Noun) A sort of flattish, round cake made of flour, with sugar, salt, and baking-powder.

Bajan, Bajun. (Colloquial.) Ba'dian, Barbadian.

bald-plated is generally preferred to bald-pated.

ballahoo, not to be confused with ballyhoo, is the name given to the spectral dog of popular lore. The ballahoo is imagined as being the size of a calf, and its appearance is accompanied by clanking of chains. As I have been informed, *It ain't nice for nobody to see a ballahoo.*

baller. (Pronounced to rhyme with taller). The bit of stick on which the ball of string used in kite-flying is wound. Hence the expressive metaphor *out to the baller,* to the extent of one's powers.

balloon juice. A happy name for the many and variously coloured **sweet drinks** that are so popular on the market nowadays.

ball-starch. Cassava starch squeezed into a ball by hand, and sold by hucksters.

bank. (Verb) To enjoy oneself on a bank holiday, usually be going on some outing. *I hear you were out banking Easter Monday.*

banka, bunka. A sore or injured foot or leg wrapped in bandages is sometimes referred to as a banka, or bunka, foot.

banjo. The term **play** banjo (together with **took**) is sometimes used in a special sense, as *Child, don't let me hear you play any took and banjo today, Sunday.* To sing, whistle, or hum any secular air.

banquet. Pronounced in the Barbadian manner (see **PRO NUNCIATION**) with the former syllable accentuated and the voice rising on the second, the **banquet** is a delicious little confection made of peanuts, and sold only, as far as I am aware, at the Women's Self-Help Shop.

Barbados. Often spelt Barbadoes, and too often mispronounced Bubbayduss. The following terms from the S.O.E.D. may prove of interest since some of them are now obsolete:— "Barbado(e)s **cherry,** the tart fruit of the Malphigia urens; Barbado(e)s **leg**, a form of elephantiasis; Barbado(e)s **nuts,** the purgative seeds or fruits of the Curcas purgans; Barbado(e)s **pride**, poinciana pulcherrima, used for fences; Barbado(e)s **tar**, a greenish petroleum; Barbado(e)s **water**, a cordial flavoured with orange and lemon-peel. Barbado(e)s, (verb) to transport to Barbados". Many extravagant claims have recently been made about the vitamin content of the cherry, which continues, like the Barbados pride, to flourish; the nut is probably the **physic** nut *(see Bush Teas of Barbados)*, and like the leg, the tar, and the water are now only memories; so is the use of the verb.

bare. *He sells bare oranges,* i.e. he sells only oranges and nothing else. *When I finished the job, he give me the bare money,* (not even a drink).

bassa-bassa. General confusion, noise, and, in some cases, exchange of blows, as *Boy, when the spree over, we going make bassa-bassa.* Origin obscure; possibly an importation from Trinidad.

bat. (i) A name frequently applied to small moths and candle-flies. The true bat is known as the **leather**-bat. (ii) Bat and **ball**. Very small boys before their introduction to the game of cricket are said to play at bat and ball.

bateau. The small flat-bottomed, roughly constructed boat in which pairs of boys or young men row out to ships in harbour in order to dive for coins.

bath, bathe. The former is invariably a noun, the latter a verb. One does not bath a baby, but bathes it; one does not take a sea bathe, but a sea-bath.

bath-suit. Bathing costume.

bayhouse. A house by the sea-side rented by the month.

bay rum. A lotion (not "a perfume", C.O.D.) distilled from the bay (Pimenta acris) tree.

bayside. The sea coast, the beach.

beach. (School slang.) To kick a football high. Also to pull a beach.

bearance. Mr. Louis Lynch writes: "There is a period of social relationship... intermediate between the cessation of ordinary civilities and the declaration of that actual warfare which is usually heralded by nocturnal stone-throwing. This period is called 'being at a bearance'." *The Barbados Book*. Most probably a corruption of 'variance'.

beating. *Doctor, I got a beating in the head* would not mean that the patient had been beaten on the head, but that he was suffering from a throbbing in the head, a violent headache.

beaver. Properly "A hat made of beaver's fur... *In beaver* (Univ. slang): in a tall hat, etc., not in cap and gown" (S.O.E.D.). Until quite recently a top hat was always referred to as a beaver: *He wore his frock coat and beaver*.

becausin. Variant of because.

beef. (School slang). To tie knots in clothing, especially the sleeves of jackets and legs of trousers. If the beefing is well done, the unfortunate owner has to resort to the use of his teeth in order to slacken the knot.

beforetime. Once upon a time, formerly. *Before-time you could buy these things for half the price you are paying today.*

behave. The word "like" is frequently omitted after this verb; a child is admonished to *behave a good boy,* or *a nice girl,* as the case may be.

being is sometimes used as a conjunction meaning since. The quotation *Sir John, you loiter here too long, Being you are to take soldiers up in counties as you go (King Henry IV, Pt II, Act II, Sc. 2)* would seem to show that it was accepted as good colloquial English once, especially when it is noted that the speaker is the Lord Chief Justice. (See also **by**.)

bell(e?)-topper. (Obsolete.) A top hat.

belly. It is sufficient to say when referring to any malaise of this region *He has the belly.* (See also **bowels**). Belly **conscience**: the small white crabs, found on every beach, that convey even cigarette ends to their holes in chance of finding something to eat are thus designated. Vulgar, perhaps, but how expressive! Belly **hurt**, belly-ache.

bellyologist. (facetious). A glutton.

below. To the leeward side of. (See **above**).

be-out. Without. Occasionally used as a conjunction, as *I ain't going be-out he tell me.*

besides. *He got no manners and to besides, he is a liar.* The meaning is obvious, but why 'to besides'? Actually this is a form of the **COMPOUND REDUNDANT**, to bring a corruption of *too, and too besides.* It should be noted that the preposition *to* is pronounced *tuh.*

betsy white. The song or chirp of the black bird.

biddims. (slang). See **gun-mout's**.

big. *Very big* usually replaced by big-**able**; *a big-able man, lorry etc.* A big **man**: a prominent member of the community. Big **people**: adults, grown-ups. Big-**grain rice**. (Facetious) During the rice shortage of the war years, planters were compelled by law to grow more **ground provisions**, chief of which was the sweet potato, so that the latter took the place of the daily rice dish. Big-**foot move:** a trick, a smart dodge.

Bim. "A native of Barbados", C.O.D. The origin of this word is obscure; the following explanation taken from *George H. McLellan: Some Phases of Barbadian Life, 1909* seems better than most: "A letter appeared in the *Daily Argosy* (Demerara) asking the origin of the word Bim, applied to mean a Barbadian, and of **Bimshire**, a name designated to Barbados. Another writer in reply to the question threw out the suggestion that the word Bim was a corruption of Byam, a Royalist leader of fire-eating fame, who figured conspicuously in the stirring epoch of Barbados history, 1650—1652, when the colonists, true to the Royalist cause, declared for King Charles, and from the 16th October, 1651, to the 11th January, 1652, defended the island from the blockading fleet of the Commonwealth. The same writer suggested further that the followers of Major Byam became known as Bims, and gradually, as the term was used in less restricted sense, to mean all Barbadians, so in like manner Barbados was called Bimshire, these names, however, being never seriously applied".

Bimshire. See **Bim** above.

birdspeed. Very fast. *He went down the road birdspeed.*

biscuit. (Anatomical) The patella or knee-cap.

bissick. To give someone the bissick signifies to make someone suffer. Probably a reference to Bissex Hill, but I have not been able to trace the connection.

bit, bitt. "In the Southern States of N. America, etc., a small silver coin forming a fraction of the Spanish dollar, or of its value in current money 1863", S.O.E.D. Actually "in the absence of an adequate supply of small coins Barbados and other colonies adopted the practice of cutting the silver dollar into eight equal segments which were known as 'bitts'. From this practice... descended the custom of using 'bitt' as a currency denomination although there never was a sterling coin of corresponding value". Dr. Ida Greaves: *Money and Currency in Barbados. Journal of the B.M.H.S., Vol. XX, No.1.* Until the recent rise in prices, certain articles of the huckster's stock were always sold by the bitt *Eggs three for the bit, Flying fish four for the bit,* etc. The bit was ten cents, but in British Guiana eight cents.

bitch. A term of abuse by no means confined to the female sex. Also used as a verb, as, *The tailor completely bitched up my new suit*; that is, spoilt it. The present participle can be best defined by an example: a *bitching*-headache. See also **black bitch**.

bite. To itch, as, *My toes biting me too bad*.

black. Found in many compounds; black**bitch**: a kind of sweet-meat made from dark brown sugar; black**eyes**: the small pea (Vigna catjang) which has a black spot at point of attachment to pod: black**ground**: land cleared of cane and trash for intermediate crops; black**guard** is still used as a verb, offenders are convicted in the courts for *blackguarding on the highway*: "to abuse or revile in scurrilous terms" (1784) S.O.E.D.; black **hat** (slang), occurs in the expression to *behave*, or **get on** like a black hat, i.e. to conduct oneself in an ungentlemanly or uncouth manner; black**lead** is always a lead pencil (see **lead**); black-**pot**: soot; black **sea egg**, see **cobbler** and **sea egg**; black-**soldier**: a term formerly applied to the rank and file of the old B.W.I. Regiment stationed at St. Ann's Garrison.

black up: to blacken, as *His face was all blacked up*.

blam is a portmanteau word formed from slam and bang, as, *The door just blammed*.

blend. To join with someone in a financial enterprise, especially in the buying of sweepstake tickets, etc., as, *Come lewwe blend in this race*.

blou'. A blouse: not only a woman's upper garment, but also a man's jacket. Pronounced to rhyme with plough.

blue-duppy. A bruise or black and blue on the hand or wrist caused by a blow from a cricket ball.

boar. In addition to the combinations boar-**hog** and boar-**pig** (see **COMPOUND REDUNDANT**), boar-**cat**, boar-**rat** are common.

bobo. (Nursery). A slight abrasion.

body. (Cf. Scots "Gin a body"). A person. *Hey, I didn't recognise the body was you,* or *I was the body who did it.* Body **line** (slang) (i) a sort of **heavybread**; (ii) woman's backside.

boiling house. The large building on the old sugar plantation in which the cane juice was boiled to crystallisation. Boiling house **bub**: a drink concocted of rum, egg, and **sweet liquor**.

bonny-clabber. "Milk naturally clotted on souring. 1631" S.O.E.D.

boo. (Verb). Applicable to flies swarming on some object, as, *Don't let the flies boo on your food.* (Noun) Usually in the plural; mucus from the eyes or nose. See also **bugaboos.**

bookkeeper. Usually the assistant to the manager on a sugar estate.

bosie. No doubt from the U.S. bo: old fellow, old boy.

bo'sun. Formerly, man in charge of "feeding" the rollers of the old wind-mills with canes. His was a position of responsibility, since he had also to keep an eye out for approaching squalls, and issue orders for moving the **points** out of the wind.

botsy. Backside.

box and dice. Chequered, or patterned with squares of alternating colour. The term is also applied to fields that have been ploughed in rectangular pots.

box cart. Made by the simple expedient of attaching an axle and wheels and a pair of short shafts to any box that is big and strong enough, the box cart is usually the handiest way for small boys to carry household vessels to the standpipe for water, or to carry small loads.

boy. Often, a servant. See **cow**-boy, **garden**-boy, **leader**-boy, **yard**-boy. Boy**child**, see **COMPOUND REDUNDANT**.

bram. (Slang). A small dancing party not pretentious enough to be styled a ball. Hence bram **house,** a small dance hall.

brass up. (Slang) *The sergeant brassed up his men when he heard they had let the prisoner escape,* i.e. gave them a good "dressing down".

brave. Still frequently used in its Elizabethan sense, as, *He's a brave little fellow* (He's a fine little boy), or *He made some brave strokes in his score of 85* (recent cricket commentary).

bread. Frequently used to mean a loaf. *Buy two breads at the shop for me.* Bread**kind** is a pleasant, housewifely sort of word applied to any starchy foods, as *I hope my wife send a lot of bread-kind with the meat.* Bread and **cheese**: an evergreen plant which forms an excellent hedge. It bears twisted reddish pods that contain jet black seeds with sometimes white, sometimes red, pulp attached.

breadfruit-swopper. A cheap, ordinary sort of person.

breakfast. Properly the first meal of the day, though most Barbadians take *early* or *morning tea.* The breakfast hour in Bridgetown may be at any time between the hours of 11 a.m. and 2 p.m.

break fives. Colloquial expression for *put it there, shake hands.*

Breakwater, The. What is now the Esplanade, Bay Street.

brew. To pour hot milk, tea, etc. back and forth from one vessel to another for the purpose of cooling it.

bride. The expression *I ain't no bride* means "I am no model of good behaviour," and has no reference whatever to the marital state.

brief. A begging letter. Some unfortunate having lost all his possessions by fire or other mishap or being incapacitated from work, gets some well-known person in the community to state the facts on a sheet of foolscap, and armed with this, he solicits alms. Briefs usually have a long life, and are discarded only when they disintegrate.

bring down. (Slang). To cause unpleasantness. *What you doing going to bring down a* **big-able** *row*.

broadroad. Highway.

brox. To strike one stone or brick with another, a small boy's game. Used metaphorically, as at a game of cricket: *We can brox them down for under fifty*.

bruise. Always used to mean an abrasion and never with its correct meaning, a contusion, except in the term **stone-bruise**.

brush. Sometimes means to file, as, *Lend me a file to brush this saw*. Brush **off:** *We brush off now: we ain't friends no more*. Such a statement is frequently accompanied by a gesture as of brushing something off the hands.

bubbies. Female breast.

bucket a drop. Certainly a much more expressive and sensible phrase to denote a heavy fall of rain than the trite and absurd cats and dogs.

buck pot. A bowl-shaped iron pot formerly manufactured with a skillet-like handle. Buck pots are imported and invoiced as Danish pots.

Buckra. See **backra**.

budge-mouth. Bird-mouth, an interior or re-entrant angle cut out of the end of a piece of timber.

bugaboos. See **boos**.

Building, The. The Government or Public Buildings in Bridgetown are thus usually referred to. The word may also be used as an

adjective, as *I met him in the Building yard,* or *I have* (pointing to
watch) *Building time.* The large clock facing Trafalgar Square has
been singularly accurate since its installation 100 years ago.
building. (Verb). *The rain building,* that is, clouds are building
up or massing, it's going to rain.

bull. A slip of paper attached to a kite to produce a humming
sound when in flight. Cf. bull-roarer.

bull-cow. There is no implication of hermaphroditism; in rural
districts a bull is sometimes thus designated.

bull in a cork hat. A few years ago, with the advent of the artificial
insemination of cattle, inspectors of the Sanitary Department were
sent around to perform the operation. These inspectors always
wore 'cork hats', i.e. sun helmets. One of the inspectors having
been assured that the cow in question was quite docile, received a hard
kick from the animal when he attempted to perform the operation. On
his expostulating angrily on this disaster, he was informed by the
owner: *You must remember this cow never see a bull in a cork hat
before.*

bull pizzle. The S.O.E.D. states under the second word of this
compound, still in current use locally: "Now *dial,* or *vulgar,* 1523...
The penis of an animal; often that of a bull, used as a flogging
instrument".

bum-by. Possibly a corruption of 'bye and bye', presently, as, *I'll see
you bumby, soon as I finish what I doing.*

bung-navel, pronounced bung-nable, is a protuberant navel.

bupp. (Nursery). To bump one's head on something.

burn. "To sting, bruise, hurt (of a poisonous insect or plant; even
of the effect of ice): *That lump of ice burn my mouth." Harrisonian,
Dec., 1924.* Tight shoes are always said to burn one's feet. The
expression to burn a **grain** signifies to go at full speed.

burying. A funeral.

burying-ground. The spot where a person is buried, or a church yard or cemetery. A very common expression is *To curse someone past his burying-ground,* i.e., to damn him to eternity.

'buse. (Abuse.) To use abusive language, as, *They was 'busin' each other in the broad road the worst way. But he can 'buse bad though, nuh!*

bush. Plants and shrubs are divided roughly into three categories: flowers, which mainly comprise roses, carnations, anthuriums and other varieties of cultivated lilies; bush, which includes other plants grown in a garden — marigolds, zinnias, etc., and wild bush, which includes all other forms of vegetation except trees and weeds.

bush-bath. A bath in which mainly herbs have been steeped. There are two types of bush-bath; one for the curing of chronic illnesses of some sort, and the other "to change one's luck when the affected one finds it difficult to meet the demand of insistent creditors or is crossed in love." For further particulars, see Mr. Louis Lynch's *The Barbados Book.*

bush tea. A watery infusion of some plant or herb. The names of many of these plants may excite interest: Gully-root, Three fingers, Bellyache-bush, Miraculous bush, Congo-eye, Do-ra-me bush, Bitter-tally, Duppy basil, etc. Mrs. Iris Bayley's article, *The Bush Teas of Barbados (Journal B.M.H.S., Vol. XVI, No. 3)* is quite comprehensive.

Bushe time. The experiment of daylight-saving time, carried out during the war (1942-3), so called as Sir Grattan Bushe was the Governor.

business. Domestic servants are referred to as *being in business. That don't business me:* That is no concern of mine.

busylickum. A busybody.

butler. A maid servant who waits at table is often thus pretentiously styled.

butt. (Verb.) (i) Butt **up** (cf. run into), to meet by accident, as, *I butt up on George in town yesterday* (ii) butt **out** is used in directing someone to a place, as, *if you follow this street, you will butt out on the main road* (iii) butting (a)**bout:** trying to find one's way, as, *There I was butting 'bout in the dark.*

buttery. (Pronounced buttry) According to the C.O.D. a buttery is "a place in colleges where bread & ale, butter, &c. are kept." The store-room in the old plantation houses where yams, potatoes, cornmeal etc., were kept.

by. Often used as a conjunction, since. *By I was home sleeping I didn't hear about the fire till next morning.*

C.

cabbage tree. The cabbage palm (Oreodoxa oleracea) which often attains a height of 100 feet.

cabin. A rough bed made of a pallet of straw placed upon a plank supported by boxes. *There's no cot in the servants' room, but we can rig up a cabin for her.*

caffuffle. To confuse. *He was completely caffuffled by the problem.* The word, spelt carfuffle, is found in Northern English dialect.

cahn. For can't: see **CLIPPING**.

cane. (seldom if ever referred to as sugar cane) occurs in the following compounds: cane-**arrow** (see **arrow**); cane-**bill** (billhook), an implement for cutting canes; cane **blade**, the leaf of the cane; cane-**butt**, the lower extremity of the cane, unfit for use in the manufacture of sugar; cane-**carrier**, endless cable which conveys canes to the rollers of the mill; cane-**cart**, a V-shaped cart formerly used for carrying cut canes to the mill-yard; cane-**fodder**, the green leaves of the cane used as such; cane-**hoist**, a large crane-like machine which conveys cut canes to the carriers (see also **scrambler**); cane-**hole**, (see **hole**) small area allocated to the planting of (usually a pair) cane-**plants**; cane-**meat** (see meat), cane-fodder; cane-**peeling**, the hard rind which must be stripped off with a knife (or, more usually, with the teeth) in order to suck the cane; cane-**piece**, (see **piece**), a cane-field; cane-**plant,** the upper portion of the cut cane which is planted to produce a fresh crop; cane **sparrow**, "the smaller of our two sparrows, greener in colour than the large sparrow. The male has the head, breast, and belly smoky black" *Mrs. Anderson: Birds of Barbados*; cane-**weigher**, an official appointed to weigh canes in a factory. Cane-**trash**, listed in the C.O.D. as "stripped leaves of sugar-cane used as fuel", is also used for mulching, and as litter for animals. **Lady** cane, a slim long-jointed cane. The **man in** the canes, an outlaw, vagabond, or bogey: *If you behave naughty, the man in the canes will come for you.*

care. (Verb transitive.) To take great care of. *You must care your books,* or *She cared all the children like a mother.*

careen. Owing to some confusion perhaps with the word "career" ("Of a horse. A short gallop at full speed... 1764". S.O.E.D.) the word is still commonly used in this sense, as, *He went careening down the road without even noticing us.*

carry. Frequently used to mean, to bring or take a person or animal somewhere; *Carry the cow to the pen for me.* To carry **away** is a euphemism for to steal: *His companions carried away all his money.*

carpet muster. (See **throw up**). A collection of (usually) "coppers", a subscription made on the spot.

cartoon is preferred to "carton"; e.g *a cartoon of cigarettes.*

cast. A handful. In counting limes, okras, etc., a handful of five is called a cast.

cast up. Throw up, vomit.

cat. See **sea-cat**. Cat-**hook** or cat-**iron**: a fish-spear or harpoon used in catching sea-cats. Cat-**wire**: barbed wire.

cat-boil. A stye on the eyelid. Cat-boils are popularly supposed to be caused when the sufferer has taken back into his possession something he has given someone else. In the first edition of these *Notes* I observed: "The reference to cat is obscure, though I have been told that the cat-boil may be cured by the application of a cat's tail or whiskers." Since then I came across the following extract in T.H. Snow's *The Scandalmongers*. It is an excerpt from the diaries of the Rev. James Woodforde, who was Vicar of Weston, Norfolk, during the latter years of the eighteenth century: "Mar. 11, Friday (1791)... Mem. The Stiony (stye) on my right Eye-lid still swelled and inflamed very much. As it is said that the eye-lid being rubbed by the tail of a black cat would do it much good if not entirely cure it, and having a black Cat, a little before dinner I made a trial of it, and very soon after dinner I found my Eye-lid much abated of the swelling and almost free from Pain. I cannot but therefore conclude it to be of the greatest service to a Stiony on the Eye-lid". **cat passion**. A little fit of temper. *Child, don't get into none of your cat passions with me.*

cat teeth. A stitch used in sewing so called on account of its resemblance to cat's teeth.

catch oneself. The phrase of returning from day-dreaming to actuality is described, not inappropriately, as catching oneself.

catercorner. Placed diagonally, especially with reference to the position of furniture in a room, as, *Let's put the wardrobe catercorner.* From *cater*, the number 4 on cards or dice.

catspraddle. Facetious form of spraddle.

c'dear, cuh-dear. One of the most common exclamations, apparently peculiar to Barbadians. It is used with a variety of shades of meaning, the most usual being (i) to express a certain degree of impatience or remonstrance, as, *C'dear, you ain't ready yet?* Very often, mixed with this impatience, is to be detected a certain disappointment, or even disgust, though the general impression is that the words are spoken more in sorrow than in anger, as, *C'dear, man, you mean to tell me you don't know no better than that?* (ii) To express a request of some sort, in which an appeal is made to the better nature of the person addressed, as *C'dear, don't hit him so hard,* or, *C'dear, Mummy, give me another piece of cake, nuh!* (iii) To express sympathy towards some unfortunate, or even on hearing bad news, as, *Cuh-dear, he only got one eye,* or, *He loss everything in the fire? Cuh-dear:* (iv) An expression of spontaneous delight occasioned by some sight, such as that of a baby; child, or bride, as would appeal to the maternal instinct, as, *Cuh-dear, ain't she sweet, though!* I had stated in the first edition of these *Notes* that the phrase was "obviously a corruption of 'good dear', but it would appear that this was, to say the least, a rash conclusion. The derivation of the phrase is still a matter of conjecture, both the following claims deserving consideration: (i) that it is a corruption of the French phrase *Que dire* (What can I say?), or (ii) that it derives from the Elizabethan oath *What the good year!* There is much to be said in favour of (i), the Barbadian schoolboy would pronounce the French phrase in exactly the same way, Cuh-dear; but it seems odd that this should be the only Gallicism to have become so intimate a part of our dialect. As regards (ii), it may prove interesting to examine its history and its use a little more closely. Good year (also written good-yer, good-yere, goodjer, goodier), was "apparently used as a meaningless expletive in 'what the good year' ... supposed by some, without evidence, to be a word originally meaning 'the French disease' " (C.T. Onions: *A Shakespeare Glossary*). Ignoring its unsavoury origin, a matter of conjecture anyway, let us take some examples from Shakespeare: (i) "On my word, captain, there's none such here. What the good-year! do you think I would deny her?" — *King Henry IV: Part II*; (ii) "What the good-year, my lord! why are you thus out of measure sad?" — *Much Ado about Nothing:* (iii) "Sir, the maid loves you, and all shall be well. We must give folks leave to prate: what the good-jer!" — *The Merry Wives of Windsor.* Now if I may venture to translate these quotations into Ba'dian, we get: (i) *Deedanfait', captain, there ain't nobody like that there. C'dear, you think I was going tell you either lie? (ii) Cud-dear, master, you looking sad enough. Why, nuh? (iii) The young woman love you. Everything going be all right. C'dear, man, you got to give people something to talk 'bout.* Which examples, I think, may weigh the scales in favour of its Elizabethan origin.

change is of course the money returned as balance of an amount tendered for an article, but it has come to be transferred to the money itself: *Please give me a piece of change.*

chat, chat down. (Slang). To engage a girl in flirtatious talk, usually with the idea of "making a date".

check. To stop, or to cause to stop: *Check the bus for me,* or *Why you don't check when I ring the bell?*

cheese. When delighted and vociferous crowds called out *Cheese, cheese!* at H.R.H. Princess Margaret during her recent visit to Barbados, she asked to be enlightened as to the meaning of the word. Actually it is listed in the C.O.D. and the S.O.E.D. as "the correct thing (prob. Anglo-Ind. *f*, Pers. & Hind *ch¹* thing,)" A correspondent writes: "In a volume of *Punch* of the 80's I have seen a Du Maurier drawing of a fashionable drawing-room and an exquisite singing.

> O ain't I the cheese, ain't I the cheese
> Out by the Serpentine under the trees
> As I stroll in the Park with my pretty Louise?"

Cheese was one of the most popular vogue-words of the 20's, and I thought it had gone the way of most of its kind until its recent revival. A cheese **boy** was a dude, a cheese **girl**, one's sweetheart.

cheese on! (Occasionally **cheese on bread!** or **chee-don!**) Expression denoting approbation or admiration.

chick. A halfpenny French loaf, now, alas, a thing of the past.

chicken and rice, young chicken and rice. A poor man's dish of rice and mustard leaves. Probably facetious in origin.

chief. (Used colloquially as a noun). Master, person in authority (U.S.) "A word with you, chief..." is the favourite gambit employed by beggars, loiterers, etc.

Chinese world. The expression 'in a Chinese world' denotes something that is quite impossible, as, *That couldn't happen in a Chinese world*. But why Chinese? Is it connected in any way with 'Chinese puzzle', some very difficult problem, or does it refer perhaps to the popular conception of the way of life in old China a sort of topsy-turvydom as exemplified by the patient's ceasing to pay his doctor as soon as he fell ill, and so on? But the expression is very common.

chink. Bed-bug. The S.O.E.D. states: "Chinch (pronounced chinsh) 1605. (*a*. Sp. chinche) ... called also chinch-, Chink-bug, Webster".

chinky. (Slang). Stingy, miserly.

chip. (Subs. and verb.) A short, quick step; to walk with short quick steps. *The batsman took two or three chips down the pitch to meet the ball half-volley. There goes the old man, chipping along. The boss had his secretary chipping* would imply that the boss having discovered some mistake on the secretary's part was giving him a very uncomfortable half-an-hour.

Cholera. An epidemic of cholera in 1854 when some 20,000 of the population died. This incident was used by the peasantry as a means of establishing dates: *I was born in Cholera,* or *I was a little girl in Cholera.* (See also **The Dust**, and **The Storm**.)

chooka-chooka. (Slang). Echo word for an old motor car.

Christmas. The common cold is anything but seasonal; however, colds that afflict Barbadians during the month of December are known as Christmas colds; Christmas **breeze**; at this time there is a slight fall in temperature along with the return of the trade winds; Christmas **worm**: small spiky black worm very prevalent during the month of December.

chuck. In addition to its meanings in Standard English, the word is also used to describe the rough push that is so often the invitation to a fight.

chuck up. Variant of chock, very close to. *He was sitting chuck up next to* (or, *on top of) me.*

chupse. A sound made by pouting the lips and sucking in air between the teeth; indicative of distrust or sulking. Mr. Richard Allsopp in *The Language we Speak (Kyck-over-al, October,* 1950) writes; "words exist in West and East African languages which contain a sound produced by sucking air between the teeth. What connection this may have with sulking or defiance, however, as it does in our (British Guiana) dialect, I do not know." The form of the word varies: some prefer **stupse**: also **suck one's teeth**. I was taken severely to task by the leader writer of the *Advocate* over this rather colourless definition. He wrote: "This may be true, but how inexpressive! The chupse is not a word, it is a whole language. There is the small effortless chupse of indifference; the thin hard chupse of mere disdain; the long, liquid, vibrating chupse which shakes the rafters and expresses every kind of defiance. It is the universal language of the West Indies, the passport to confidence from Jamaica to British South America. How dare the compiler degrade it to a mere word!" I can only say very humbly that I stand rebuked; and hope that the following classification may do something towards mollifying the dissatisfaction of the critic: (i) the chupse of AMUSED TOLERANCE used in retort to some absurd remark or statement, a sort of oral shrugging of the shoulders: (ii) the chupse SELF-ADMONITORY, when the chupster has done something of which he has no occasion to be proud; (iii) the chupse DISDAINFUL, accompanied by a raising of the eyebrow; (iv) the chupse DISGUSTED in the performance of which the eyelids are almost closed; (v) the chupse SORROWFUL, in reality a series of quickly emitted chupses, the head being shaken slowly from side to side; (vi) the chupse OFFENSIVE or ABUSIVE; (vii) the chupse PROVOCATIVE, a combination of iii, iv, and vi, which often leads to blows. But even this enumeration, I fear, is not comprehensive.

clean out. This term is often used to express early dawn; see also **foreday morning**. *And when day clean out I was already on the way to the beach.*

clear-skinned. Applied to complexion: light or yellowish brown.

clerkess. This feminine form of the noun, clerk, is, as far as I know, used nowhere else. It does not however mean a lady-clerk, but a female shop-attendant.

CLIPPING. It may be taken as a general rule that final d's and t's immediately following a consonant (except l and r) are not pronounced. Thus one hears *ac, fac, contrac,* for act, fact, contract; *sof* for soft; *san, lan, gran,* for sand, land, grand; *poun* and *groun* for pound and ground: *fas* and *las* for fast and last; and so on. A curious and interesting situation arises when the negative form of "can" is thus clipped: how is it to be distinguished from its affirmative? This is accomplished by lengthening the vowel sound of the former, as, *You cahn live for ever*, as opposed to the shortened vowel sound of the latter, as, *You kin dead at any time.*

clips. Pince-nez.

closet. Never a recess for storing clothes, etc.; always a small outhouse-latrine, a privy; also referred to as an earth-closet to distinguish it from the w.c.

coalpot. The coalpot which is to be found in almost every home is, of course, not a pot at all. But nobody ever refers to it by its proper name, a Dutch stove.

cob. (Rare). A word applied to a person (usually) of mixed African and Indian blood. The skin is very dark and **smooth**, the hair black and almost **good.**

cobbler. (i) The long-spiked, black sea-urchin; also known as the black **sea-egg.** (ii) The frigate or man-'o-war bird occasionally "seen sailing high up on outstretched slender wings, and easily identified by (its) black colour (with a white crescent on the breast of the female) and very long forked tail" *Mrs. Anderson: Some observations on the Birds of Barbados. (The Journal of the B.M.H.S., Vol. II, Nos. 2 and 3.)*

cock lizard. The larger green lizard is often thus named, not only I fancy, on account of considerations of sex, but owing to the fact that it often displays its yellow gills which hang from beneath its throat like a cock's wattles.

cock-loft. (Facetious). A small bedroom in the upper storey of a house. Cf. "Small upper loft usually reached by a ladder 1589". S.O.E.D.

cocksies. When a spun coin falls edgewise, it is said to be cocksies. Probably cognate with **cock up.**

cock up. A Berbice chair is ideal seat for cocking up one's legs, but a near-by window-sill, desk, etc., is the more usual way of enjoying this means of relaxation. Cock up one's **heels**: assume an attitude of indifference. (Metaphorical).

cocobay. "A type of leprosy with an African name... (Twi*cocobe*)." Frederic G. Cassidy: *Jamaica Talk.* 1961. The word is now rarely used in Barbados. I am told it was also applied to certain types of ulcerous skin-disease.

cohobbleopot. (Colloquial) A stew composed of a variety of ingredients.

cold. "The Barbadian applies the term *cold* to a large variety of unrelated diseases. Diarrhoea and dysenteric disorders are *a cold in the bowels:* cystitis, *a cold in the bladder*: headache, *a cold in the head*: lumbago and back pain, *a cold in the back*. Almost any disease can thus be classified as a cold, whilst the common or garden cold, or coryza, is dignified by the term **fresh cold.**" *Iris Bayley: The Bush Teas of Barbados, (The Journal of the B.M.H.S., Vol. XVI, No.3).*

cold drawn oil. Locally prepared castor oil.

collar. A coconut "bread" shaped like collar or yoke of a woman's blouse.

collective is often used instead of collected, in the sense of calm, not distracted; as, *In spite of all his trouble, he seemed quite collective.*

come round. (Slang). *The gang got hold of him and make him come round,* i.e., gave him all that was coming to him.

comfort. Probably a corruption of comfit, but used only to refer to locally made sticks of peppermint.

coming. (Adjective). Expressing future time, as *I'll see you Friday coming,* or, *The concert is Friday coming week.*

commanding powder. A powder having the potency of a love potion.

common. It may be noted that the term, common, as applied to pens, serves to distinguish them from fountain pens; and to pins, to distinguish them from safety pins.

compliment, when pronounced with exaggerated emphasis on the first syllable, (see **PRONUNCIATION**) is an invitation to a wedding. See also **hymeneal.**

COMPOUND REDUNDANT. There are quite a few of these unusual formations. There may be excuse for some of them, e.g., **boar-hog,** when it is borne in mind that the word *boar* is used to distinguish the male cat, and rat; **ram sheep,** when the male goat is called a **ram-goat**; **fowlcock,** when *cock* is applicable to many male birds; but there seems to be little that can be said for such redundancies as **boychild** (male child), **doll-baby** (doll), **gate-door** (gate), **hare-rabbit** (hare), **sow-pig** (sow), **sparrow-bird** (sparrow), **rockstone** (stone). Also deserving of mention are **to(o) besides** (besides), **back-back** (to go back), **out-out** (extinguish), **play-play** (make-believe), **wee-wee** (tiny, wee,) etc.

conaree. A large glazed earthenware vessel in which meat is corned, pickled, or cooked. "Being thick, it is suited to foods requiring long, slow cooking such as stews." (*West Indian Cookery: E. Phyllis Clark*). Also spelt **canaree.**

conceited. Occasionally used in the sense of dumbfounded, as, *Man, the thing (occurrence) had me conceited.*

concern. *This young woman concern you?* or, *That child concerning me* will suffice as examples for the use of this word, which implies having an interest in someone.

confirmation bow tie. "The origin of the term is obscure, but the signs of the disorder are distressingly apparent. It is a by-product of dyspepsia, and the corners of the mouth of the sufferer temporarily lose their pigmentation and become white." Louis Lynch: *The Barbados Book.*

conkie. Perhaps it would be best to give the recipe for this delicacy: "Beat six eggs lightly, and add to them 4 ozs. sugar, 8 ozs., pumpkin which has been previously boiled and mashed, 10ozs. butter, ½ pint milk, 1 lb. cornflour and 1 grated coconut. Mix well, flavour with nut-meg, and put a large spoonful of the mixture on pieces of **quailed** plantain leaf. Fold up carefully and steam over boiling water for one hour or more. Turn out the leaves, pour over melted butter and serve." *(A Souvenir of Barbados: compiled by Gladys Skinner)*. In many households conkies are traditionally served on the fifth of November.

coo-coo, couscous. A standard dish. Here is the recipe for cornmeal coo-coo from *W.I. Cookery: E. Phyllis Clark:* 'Wash and slice ochroes (sic), add salt, and boil them in half the liquid. When the ochroes are soft enough to be swizzled, mix the cornmeal with the rest of the liquid. Stir this paste into the boiling liquid and continue to cook, stirring all the time until the mixture is thick and smooth. Turn out into well-buttered mould or basin'. Coo-coo is also made from Indian corn, guinea corn, breadfruit, bananas, yams, potatoes, etc. etc.

coob. (Noun). A corruption of coop, "A cage or pen of basketwork or the like for confining poultry:" S.O.E.D. The local coob is, however, always constructed from boxes and bits of board; usually referred to as a fowl- or pigeon-coob. Properly, a hutch.

cooling-tea. A febrifuge of herbs.

cool out. To sit at one's ease, especially on a verandah, enjoying the breeze, or else doing nothing in particular, idling. *Look at we all working and he at home cooling out!*

coppers. (Slang). In addition to meaning copper coins, the word is also used in a sense similar to spondulicks, dough, etc.: as *He can buy a car; he got the coppers.*

cork hat. A sun helmet.

cork-sticking. A schoolboy's rough and tumble game. Given a tennis ball and some elbow-room, two or three dozen youngsters learn to improve their aim, as well as to get out of the way quickly.

corn. (Verb). To acquire in plenty. (Corn in Egypt?) *Since he start keeping shop he corning the money.* (Or cornering?)

corn and oil. A drink compounded of rum and **falernum**.

corn bird. See **cow bird.**

cornrip. (Vulgar). More genteel colloquialisms seem to be replacing this racy, forthright word which used to be applied to a prostitute. (Common rip?)

cotton-tree. The upland plover; so called because it feeds on the parasitic caterpillars of the cotton plant.

couple. Almost always a few. *Boy, squeeze me a couple of limes — About three, sir? — Better make it four.*

courting nuts. Peanuts.

cow. The following compounds may be noted: cow **bird,** "a smoky grey bird of the size of the blackbird... it has a beautiful hubbling cry, generally uttered on the wing (Molothrus bonariensis)" *Mrs. Anderson*: *Some observations on the Birds of Barbados;* cow**boy**, a boy who helps to wash, feed, and milk cows; cow-**cart**, heavy cart drawn by oxen; cow **itch**, cowage, Macuna pruriens, whose pods are covered with stinging hairs; cow**minder**, a cowherd; cow**skin**, a cowhide; cow **swopper**, one who speculates in the buying and selling of cattle and other live stock (see **speculator**). **Woman** cow, a free-martin. See also **kill** cow.

crab. (Verb). To catch crabs; hence, **crabber,** one who catches crabs. For an account of **crabbing**, see the delightful chapter *If Crab no Walk*, in Louis Lynch's *The Barbados Book*.

crab-dog. The racoon, now believed to be extinct in Barbados.

crab-mash. To iron clothes badly. Creases formed through bad ironing are known as **duppy tucks**.

crapaud. One of the very few French words in common usage: a toad (Bufo marinus). The word toad is never used; crapaud or **frog** always.

creature. If you were told "A creature out there to you", what would you go expecting to encounter? A woman, certainly, and most likely, a poor, old, and infirm one. But the word is also applied to the sturdiest of hucksters, as, *The creature with the tomatoes call for the* **change**.

crocus, crocus-bag. Burlap, coarse canvas made of jute and hemp used for bagging. It would be interesting to discover how *crocus*, ((i) plant, (ii) saffron, (iii) a peroxide of iron) S.O.E.D. came to be applied to coarse bagging. Is it too fanciful to suggest it may be a corruption of Corchorus, the plants Corchorus capsularis and Corchorus olitorius furnishing the fibre known as jute?

crop-over. The festival to celebrate the successful harvesting of the sugar cane crop. Cf. the English harvest home.

crop-time. The season of the reaping of the sugar cane crop.

crop wind. The strong trade winds prevalent during the crop season, on which the windmills depended for grinding the cane.

cross-comical. Applied to persons in the way of good-humoured abuse, as, *Look at that cross-comical son of a so-and-so.*

cruel. (Slang.) Angry, or, not to be trifled with. *When he heard the news, he got cruel. He can be a cruel batsman when he gets ready.*

cuffin, cuffum. (Noun), (i) A somersault. Cuffins are always skinned. *All the boys were down on the beach skinning cuffins* (turning somersaults). (ii) The tarpon.

cure. (i) Of sugar. Curing is the name of the process by which the molasses is separated from the sugar. The **curing house** was the place where this took place. Formerly the sugar was placed in hogsheads with perforated bottoms and the molasses dripped out into cisterns underneath. Nowadays centrifugal machinery is used (ii) "(Of wood). To season. (iii) (Of rum.) To mature." *The Harrisonian:* July, 1926.

curing house. See **cure**, above:

29

cut. A castrated animal is said to be cut. *This is a pretty little kitten; you should have him cut.*

cut and contrive. To inch and pinch. *You don't know I does have to cut and contrive to keep these children of mine at school.*

cut down. (Noun). Slang term applied to a small, or half, bottle of rum. See **halfie.** (Adjective). Conspicuously short in stature, as *Who is that little, cut-down fellow you were talking to?*

cute. In some districts this word conveys quite the opposite meaning to the accepted use, thus, *I never see nobody look so cute*, would imply that the person referred to presented a rather ridiculous appearance.

cutlash. A cutlass.

cut (one's) eyes. When one cuts an acquaintance, one ignores him, tries to avoid meeting his eyes; the insult is given indirectly. But when one cuts one's eyes at an acquaintance, the latter is under no misapprehension: the eyes are fixed upon him in a stony glare, then after an unmistakable closing of the eyelids and a supercilious raising of the eyebrows, the glance passes on elsewhere. Also, to regard contemptuously or with disdain.

cut-plate. Bits of broken chinaware are to be found everywhere, and when one side is coloured and the other plain, what more efficient substitute for a coin in a game of **backyard cricket?**

cuts. Occasionally used to mean book-illustrations of any kind.

cutter. A small French loaf with a slice of ham, meat, or cheese inserted sandwich-fashion. Hence ham-cutter, etc.

cutting, or more usually, a cutting in the bowels: **griping.**

D.

dan-dan. (Nursery) A child's dress.

dark-eyes. To be suffering from the dark eyes is to be afflicted by spells of dizziness, or faintness.

daru. (slang.) Rum. A Hindu word.

dead. (Noun). A dead person, a corpse. *The first time I ever see a dead. This is where they bury the deads.* (Verb). Often used instead of "die", as, *He look like he going to dead soon.*

dead-house. Mortuary.

dead sand. Sand above high-water mark. *Child, don't play up in that dead sand.*

deaf-bell. A ringing noise in the ear.

deednfait. Indeed and faith. An asseveration of honesty, as, *Deednfait I wouldn't do such a thing.*

Denis. *If he takes a dislike to you, boy, you name Denis.* That is, you're in for trouble. Why Denis? I may mention that this saying was prevalent long before the appearance of the Denis of the popular cartoons.

destroyful. Destructive.

dig down. Demolish. *They digged down the building.*

dignity. Dignities or dignity balls were much in favour in the time of Sir Evan Macgregor (c. 1837) who brought a mulatto mistress from Dominica, and it is even said that a dignity ball was held at Government House in his time. They were attended by social gentlemen (not ladies) and the demi-monde. But the dignities usually took place at Caroline Lee's and other Bridgetown hotels.

dildoes. "Tree or shrub of the genus Cereus, natural order Cactaceae. 1696." S.O.E.D. But the **Flat-hand** dildoes of Barbados are of the genus Opuntia.

dip. Eddoes and shad are sometimes called **slip** and **dip.**

disimprove. Now regarded as incorrect, but listed in the S.O.E.D. as "to grow worse. 1642."

dispatch. To serve a customer in a shop. *Come, come, dispatch me: I been waiting here ever so long.* The S.O.E.D. notes: "To dismiss a person after settling his business; to get rid of. Now rare".

disremember. Fail to remember.

dite. Most likely a corruption of doit (cf, spile for spoil, etc.) *Move up a dite, young man, and let the lady get a seat.* To be heard on any bus at any time.

do. (i) To act or behave. *I never see anybody do so bad at a party.* (ii) To treat: *You do me as you like.* (iii) Often used as a notional verb, as *What do you?* i.e. What ails you? (iv) The past participle is often used in the sense of *finished: He done fishing* means he has finished, given up the occupation of catching fish. (v) The phrase *a done man*, may be noted in this connection: a full-grown man. (vi) The auxiliary *do* was used in the sixteenth century in the formation of present and past tenses without any idea of emphasis: *Who does beguile you, who does do you wrong?* and *I did send A ring ... in chase of you (Twelfth Night)* exemplify this use which is still current in Barbados. But in addition to these tenses which have at least the aura of archaisms are to be found such monstrous solecisms, as, *She does be always quarrelling, He did was to see me yesterday* (He was to have seen me yesterday), and *He did playing cricket all day.* Indeed, the past tense, *did*, is often used to replace the word was (or were), as *I did at home* (I was at home), *They did in the sea* (They were in the sea), etc., etc. To be noted also is the expression *I don't have a copy of that book* for I haven't a copy of that book. To do **up**: to launder, as, *She does up clothes very nicely:* or, to paint or otherwise decorate, as, *The house done up pretty enough.*

doctor-booby. The humming bird.

doctorshop. Chemist's shop is a term never used in Barbados; doctorshop or the more customary drugstore (U.S.) are the usual terms.

do-flicky. (Slang.) Any small tool or gadget.

dog bitters. Cure by fasting; usually prescribed for children whose appetites for some reason or other have become fastidious. *Don't want your dinner, huh? What you want is a good dose of dog bitters.*

dog-dance. To give the impression that one is deliberately shadowing or dogging the footsteps of another; thus a man who has met up with an acquaintance several times in the course of a comparatively short while might exclaim *But what you dog-dancing me for?*

dog dead. An expression of finality: all is over and done. *If he find out you lying, boy, the dog dead.*

dog-flea. The flea.

doll-baby. See **COMPOUND REDUNDANT**.

domestic. The foreigner might think that *two yards of domestic* was a facetious description of an unduly tall maid-servant; but the word is still used to mean cloth used for the lining of men's clothes. The S.O.E.D. states: "home-made cotton cloths 1622 esp. in U.S."

dominique. Applied to fowls marked like the Plymouth Rock, but of much smaller size.

dontcarish. A very useful compound for which it is difficult to find an exact synonym.

door-mouth. Threshold. *He was standing there, right in the door-mouth.*

doris. Police van, Black Maria. The couple of these motor vans used by the Police force (circ. 1938) were nicknamed Mae West and Doris, the former after the screen star and the latter after the first woman to be taken to the **main-guard** in the van.

DOUBLE NEGATIVE. This anomaly of Elizabethan days still flourishes under protest. *Somebody ain't going to get none* is a popular phrase which nicely exemplifies its use.

down, down yonder. In statements like *They've taken him down,* or *He's gone down yonder,* these adverbs become fraught with ominous significance: the person referred to has been sent to the Mental Hospital.

downalong. (Adjective). Applied to anyone from the other British West Indian islands. *But listen to she and she downalong talk. A lot of downalong people does live in that street.* Inasmuch as the syllable — *own* is almost invariably pronounced *-ung* (tung for town, etc.,), the word should be pronounced dungalong.

downfall. A snare for catching small birds.

draw. To strike a match. *These matches won't draw.*

dream. A very unusual use of this verb is often heard; someone who has dreamt of a dead relative or friend will say, for example, *My old grandmother dream me last night and tell me wasn't to have nothing to do with the business.* It will be seen that the narrator speaks of himself as having been dreamt by the deceased person who is the active agent in the matter. Is this a relic of African tribal lore?

dress down. (i) Dressed in the height of fashion; see also **geared down**. (ii) To move down in order to make room as on a bus.

drip, dripstone. a water-filter cut out of limestone. See E.M. Shilstone: *Barbados Dripstone, The Journal of the B.M.H.S., Vol. XXII, No.2.*

driver. An overseer; a relic of slavery-days when he was referred to as a slave-driver.

drop. A cake made of flour, so called because the dough is dropped on to a sheet of metal for baking.

dry food. No matter the quality or the quantity of the dish, if there is no gravy, it is referred to, somewhat derogatorily, as "dry food".

duck rest. The old saying *I wish you a duck rest* is equivalent to wishing some one a broken night's rest.

duck's guts. A somewhat unsavoury expression, denoting "in trouble"; as, *If you get catch doing that, boy, you going to be in the duck's guts.*

dumb. (Adjective). Applied to biscuits that have lost their crispness.

dumbdog. An expressive name for a schoolboy's bent pin.

duncy, duncey. Like a dunce: *The dunciest boy in the class.*

dunk. The fruit of the Zizyphus jujuba, Natural Order Rhamnaceae, very much liked by children, and a frequent cause of colic.

duppy. An apparition, a ghost. Edgar Mittleholzer in his novel, *Corentyne Thunder*, spells the word "dopie". Duppy-**agent** undertaker; duppy-**crab**, the white land crab; duppy-**dust**, bones ground to powder for purposes of Obeah: duppy-**pinch**, a black and blue of unknown cause; duppy-**umbrella**, the mushroom. See also **blue** duppy.

Dust, The. At the time of the eruption of Mont Pelèe and the Soufriere, (1902) Barbados was covered with a heavy fall of volcanic dust. Hence, *I was a little girl in the Dust.* (See **Cholera**, and **The Storm**).

dust-box. A box into which waste paper is thrown.

E.

early. The phrase *in the early* may be noted: *We got to put a stop to this in the early.*

earthless. Most probably a corruption of 'earthliest' used as an expletive, as, *I haven't one earthless cent,* or *I haven't done him the earthless thing.*

Easy Hall. The name of a sugar plantation. *To be living at Easy Hall* is the equivalent of living a life of idleness — doing no work, and being supported by someone else.

eat. Players at draughts or checkers do not take, but eat each other's men.

ECHO WORDS. Our dialect is particularly rich in Echo Words (Onomatopoeia), and these notes can offer only a few examples, since many of these words are coined from time to time, have a brief vogue, and then disappear from current use. The words in this section are all interjections, often placed next to the appropriate word or phrase to give colour to the remark. Such are **bam**, a blow or kick: *He up foot an kick the ball, bam;* **baddarax** indicates the sound of some object striking loose boards or galvanised iron, a rattling noise; **buddung** and **bruggadung**, dull, heavy noises of falling, though the former, along with **booee** and **buddooee** may also express explosions and reports of guns; **daddaie** or **haddaie** denotes glee or ridicule; **plashow**, the sound of a splash, *She empty the bucket of water over him, plashow!*; **plix**, a sharp, high-pitched sound, as *The ball hit the stumps, plix!* **plax,** a dull, smacking sound, as *The ball hit him on the jaw, plax!;* **vyee,** speedy motion, as *He went vyee, down the road.* Echo words other than interjections are noted in the list when occasion arises.

ecky-becky. Another name for the **redleg** or poor **backra**. The following bit of doggerel refers to their clannishness and refusal to mingle with the Negro population.

> Ecky-becky is a nation, true botheration:
> As you touch dem, dem run at the station.

eczemas. The plural of the word is generally used.

eddo. Plural eddoes; not listed in the the C.O.D. A tuber common to the West Indies. There are many varieties: the **Chinee** eddo, the **nut** eddo, the **tannia,** the **white** eddo and the **wild** eddo, of which only the last-mentioned is not edible. Eddo-**pippy**, the blossom of the eddo plant. **Through the eddoes,** a quaint phrase signifying that all is over; there's an end of the matter, as, *George gone through the eddoes; the magistrate sentence him this morning to three years' hard labour.*

effin. A variant of *if*. Probably formed by metathesis from *and if*.

egg flip, egg nog. The following recipe is taken from Gladys Skinner's *Souvenir of Barbados:* "One gill of milk , ½ gill of rum, one fresh egg, sugar to taste, cracked ice. Put egg in a jug and swizzle until light, add milk, rum, and sugar, and ice, and swizzle again until a good head forms. Serve at once very cold. Grated nutmeg and a dash of angostura bitters on the top makes a smart finish."

EIGHTEENTH CENTURY RELICS. "Anybody at all familiar with the Barbadian will know how he has preserved through the ages the forms of pronunciation ... which prevailed in some cases more than two centuries ago," writes the Editor of the B.M.H.S. (Vol. XXIII No. 1) "... the pronunciation of such words as 'oil', 'yellow', 'join', etc, at which highbrows may scoff is only what it must obviously have been in England two or three centuries ago. When the poet Quarles writes:—

> 'Where in a greater current they conjoin
> So I my best beloved's am: so he is mine,'

it is clear from the rhyme that the pronunciation then was what is still so commonly employed in Barbados to-day." So much for the "oil" sound of which numerous examples may be found in English verse of the eighteenth century. In words like "yellow" the short "e" is transformed into short "i", so that one may still hear such words as *trimble, kittle, umbrilla*, etc. Another eighteenth century survival is the "eck" sound in preference to the standard "ake"; so that "make", "break", "take", etc., are transformed into mek, brek, tek, etc. Cf. Pope's *Rape of the Lock*, (1714):

> Then in two sable ringlets taught to break
> Once gave new beauties to the snowy neck.

Interesting in this context is the standard pronunciation of "breakfast".

either. (Adjective). Often used to mean *any* or *a* in the same sense: *I havn't either pencil* or *You think I got either wife?* Also neither in the negative sense. Either **one** is preferred to the pronoun *either*.

ell-chamber, L-chamber. Properly a small room added at right angles to the main building, but used also to refer to any small room, perhaps because of a confusion between L and ell (45 inches).

Ellick. The phrase *late as Ellick* is proverbial, Who Ellick (Alec) was is not known.

engineer. A man operating an engine at a sugar factory.

ess. (i) Corruption of ace, as, *the ess of spades*: also used metaphorically to express excellence, as *He is the ess,* or *He knows the ess of it.* (ii) A variant of *if.*

estate. (Noun and Adjective). A sugar estate, a plantation. *The owner lives on the estate: The manager in the estate yard.*

ever, since, frequently mispronounced "every sence," a long time ago. How long may be inferred from the drawling emphasis placed on the first syllable: *That happened ehhhh-very sence. My grandfather was a boy at the time.*

except. Often used as a conjunction meaning *unless.* This function of the word (vide *Except ye be born again*) is now classified as archaic.

exhibition. (Adjective) Applied to articles of clothing, an exhibition hat, dress, etc.: a hat or dress bought to wear to the Annual Industrial Exhibition formerly held in the month of December.

expense. (Verb). To cause expense to, as, *I'm afraid owning a car would expense me too much.*

expressions. Euphemistic term for bad language. *You so young and using expressions.*

F.

factory. Always a sugar factory unless otherwise specified.

fainty. (also **fainty-fainty**). (Adjective). Faint, as *I feel fainty-*

fainty. Also used to denote a sickly odour, as, *This medicine smell too fainty-fainty.*

falernum is a local liqueur. Its exact composition is a trade secret, though two of its components are lime and sugar. Despite its pleasant taste it is extremely potent. It probably derives its name from sentimental association with Falernian, the vinum Falernum of the ancient Ager Falernus of Campania. See **corn and oil.**

fall (a)way. To lose weight. *Since he been sick, he fall way a lot.*

family. Often used to mean a relative, *That young man is family to me,* or *He is my family.*

fan. *Don't fan yourself about* is an injunction often given those recovering from illness, especially fever; i.e., Don't expose yourself to draughts, etc.

fancy basket. The fancy basket which itinerant vendors, women usually, display in and around Swan Street, contains an assortment of ribbons, thread, lace, hair-nets, combs, etc., rarely any fancy work.

farm, farmer. A woman who is employed on an estate to weed a specified area is called a farmer and her occupation is known as farming.

fash. This Scots word is occasionally used in its correct sense of bother or trouble. *Don't fash yourself.*

fashion. The phrase not in fashion is used to mean not in season, scarce. Thus, after hurricane Janet, green peas were not in fashion at Christmas time.

fassy. A corruption of chasse, a gliding step in dancing.

father. Used as a superlative. Thus, a cinema fan might refer to a film as *That is picture father, boy.*

father-giver. *I am father-giver at a wedding tomorrow;* that is, I am to give the bride away.

fat pork. The fruit of an evergreen shrub (Chrysobalamis icaco) which flourishes in the rocky soil of the "Scotland" district of Barbados. The local name of the fruit is not altogether inappropriate.

favour. *This child favours his father strong though, nuh?* "To resemble in features. Now colloq. 1605" S.O.E.D.

feature. To resemble in features; as, *That child features his father very much.*

federation. As a result of the ill-starred attempt by John Pope-Hennessy to bring about a confederation of the Windward Islands in 1876, and the consequent riots, the word federation is commonly used to refer to any noisy gathering of people, or to any quarrel in which a large number of people take part. *After the accident up the street, it was like federation,* or, *If these fellows go on annoying us, there going to be federation in the alley soon.*

feels, bad. See **bad feels.**

fever and ague. (pronounced fevernague): filaria.

fig. (i) The small "lady's finger" or silk banana. (ii) A segment of an orange. In other West Indian islands these segments are called pegs.

fine. This word carries all the usual meanings to be found in the C.O.D., but is most often used with the meaning "slender, thin, sharp, in small particles", as, fine **twine,** fine (very small) **ants.** The following incident serves as an illustration: Shortly after Hurricane Janet I met a fisherman friend of mine in town. Knowing that the district in which he lived had been hard hit by the hurricane, I asked him how he had fared, "Fine, chief," he replied, "fine." I was about to congratulate him on his good fortune, when he continued "Fine, chief. Everything mash up fine, fine, fine." The term, fine **features**, does not so much imply any degree of handsomeness, but rather of smallness.

fingersmith. A facetious term for a thief.

finny. Fin-like, withered or deformed; as, *the man with the finny hand.*

fire. (Slang.) *Come lewwe fire one* is a common invitation to have a drink, generally rum. See fire the **acid.**

fire-rage. A quarrel. *What you taking up somebody's fire-rage for?* Inasmuch as the word is applicable to women's quarrels generally, is it possible that the word is connected with *virago* spelt *firago* in Elizabethan days?

firms. (School slang). A game of cricket in which any number may take part. Two or three boys form a firm and have alternate strokes at the wicket until one of them is either caught or bowled. Then the boy who catches the ball or bowls the batsman takes his turn, along with his "firm" at the wicket.

first aid. In recent years little shops, known as first aids, have sprung up everywhere. They provide, in addition to the many patent medicines so necessary to those who have succumbed to the power of advertisement, many miscellaneous commodities.

fish. Always flying fish unless otherwise specified.

fisherman's penny. 1¹/4 cents. The following quotation , taken from Dr. Ida Greaves' comprehensive articles on *Money and Currency in the West Indies, Journal of the B.M.H.S., Vol. XX, No. 2,* may serve to throw some light on this anomaly: "In October, 1847 a Bill was introduced in the House of Assembly 'to provide for the assimilation of the Currency and Monies of Account' of Barbados to those of the United Kingdom. What this meant in effect was that the denominations of local 'current money' would disappear, and the island would count in only one set of pounds, shillings, and pence ... The Barbados currency penny had by 1848 the sanction of 'immemorial custom' and its role in reckoning prices was not readily ended by the introduction of the penny coin. The old currency value survived into the early years of this century in the term 'fisherman's penny'which was 1¹/4 cents, while 2¹/2 cents was known as 'fisherman's **tuppence'.** The general rise in prices brought about by the first World War no doubt put an end to the custom by making the value of the penny too insignificant to keep the earlier scale of reckoning prices." (See also **tuppence.**)

fish pot. A large wire cage with a funnel-shaped entrance, through which the fish find easy access and difficult, if not impossible, exit. The pots are usually taken out in boats, and, after the necessary landmarks have been taken, lowered into the deep water beyond the reef. They are hauled up periodically, and their contents are manifold. Fish caught in a fish pot are known, in distinction from deep sea fish, as **pot fish**. (Condensed from *Some Phases of Barbados Life: George H.M. McLellan.*)

fits. To give anyone fits is to annoy or embarrass him; as, *The barrister gave the witness fits during his cross examination,* or, *It gave me fits to untie that knot.*

fix. In order to avoid possible misunderstanding, should a clerk in a shop or a bank enquire of you whether you've been fixed yet, it may be useful to remember that he is politely enquiring whether you've been attended to yet.

flannin. Flannel. I suppose it would have been very difficult sixty or seventy years ago to find anyone who didn't wear "flannin." This was a garment of flannel worn next to the skin and those who refused to wear it were supposed to be tempting providence: *No wonder she catch cold exposing sheself without she flannin!* The flannin is still favoured by many of conservative temperament, and a doctor has defined it as "a heavy sweat-soaked garment worn by elderly ladies next to the skin."

flash. *If you walk around with that basin, the water will flash out.* At first sight it would appear that the speaker has been guilty of confusing the word with "splash"; but, although no longer modern Standard English, flash is listed in the S.O.E.D. as "A sudden movement of water... 1713."

flat. A vogue word of the 30's. *I was dancing flat:* I was dancing and enjoying myself to the utmost.

flat-hand dildoes. See **dildoes.**

flat-jack. A small flour cake containing grated coconut.

Fletcher. The phrase *foolish as Fletcher* is now obsolete. A certain Fletcher was said to have sawed off the limb of the tree he was sitting on.

float. Floats are small flour cakes, well blown up with baking-powder. Fish and floats are cooked on coal-pots and sold at street corners.

flurry. A flourish. Flurries may refer to the elegancies of hand-writing but may be performed with a stick or wand.

flystick. A spring operated by means of a resilient piece of wood.

foffie. An adjective applied to an eye that has a bluish-white appearance, due to lack of pigment. The word may be a corruption of *frothy.*

follow-pattern. (Adjective.) Imitative. *You too follow-pattern!*

foot. There is little or no distinction made between the foot and the leg, and the hand and the arm. Such a statement as *He got his foot broken just below the knee* is likely to prove meaningless unless this lack of distinction is borne in mind.

for. The two following uses of the word are interesting: (i) *What for a day you had?* What sort of a day did you spend, and (ii) *If you don't behave, I'll go to the Headmaster for you,* i.e., I'll report you to the Headmaster.

force-ripe. Fruit picked before it is ripe, and brought to apparent maturity by artificial means. Hence used metaphorically to mean precocious.

foreday. Usually found in the phrase foreday morning. This enchanting description of early dawn seems to have escaped the attention of poets thus far, though there is the refrain of an old folk song, *Foreday morning come and gone, And I ain't get my coffee water yet.*

Foreign. Expressed simply; non-Barbadian. Thus one buys foreign cabbage and tomatoes. Englishmen, Trinidadians and Venezuelans are all alike **foreigners.**

forenoon. Often pronounced "foonoon" is used to denote the early afternoon, and never any period of time before noon.

fortyleg. The centipede.

fountain pencil. A propelling pencil. Cf. fountain pen.

fowlcock. See **COMPOUND REDUNDANT.**

France. Often used as a mild expletive, as *Go to France* or *What the France you think you doing?* Most likely a legacy from the Napoleonic wars.

fray. Probably a corruption of *fry* (young fishes). **Blue** fray: the fry of the tarpon; **white** fray: whitebait. Fray **batter:** fray fried with flour and seasoning into small flattish cakes.

freeness. An occasion when something (particularly food and drink) is obtained without cost. *At the opening of the new cinema there was a big freeness.*

fresh. Often used in the sense of high-smelling, especially with reference to fish. Consequently in a statement like *These fish fresh enough; I ain't want none o' them,* the word conveys the exact opposite of its proper meaning.

fresh cold. See **cold.**

fret. (Noun.) Some word or nickname or action which causes annoyance to some particular person; as *The little boys have a fret on old Sam.* (Verb). Fret with: to quarrel with: to scold, as *The mistress is always fretting with the cook.*

friction. A safety match. *Mister, could you gimme a friction?*

friendsing. Only the present participle of the verb is in use: holding hands, courting; as, *They been friendsing a long time.*

frighten Friday. A timorous person. 'Friday' is possibly a corruption of 'fraidy'; indeed this other form is sometimes used.

frizzed. Applied to **salt·fish** that has been first boiled and pounded, after which it is fried with seasoning to a golden brown colour.

frizzle-fowl. A fowl with feathers lying in reverse direction to the normal.

frog. There are no true frogs in Barbados, although the common American toad (bufo marinus) is always thus designated.

front house. The front room of a labourer's cottage, the living-room.

frupse. Something of no account. *It isn't worth a frupse.*

funny-up. Odd, queer, contorted, or deformed. Extreme examples of modern art might fit into this category quite easily.

fuss-box. A fussy person.

fussy. Used with the negative to express a lack of interest or keenness, as, *I not fussy about going to pictures to-night.*

G.

galvanise. (Noun) Corrugated iron sheets coated with zinc. *The house is roofed with galvanise.*

gansy, garnsey. A woollen jersey. Corruption of Guernsey.

gap. This word has a special connotation in Barbados: the drive-way or entrance to a house. Sometimes applied to a short road, as St. Lawrence Gap, Aquatic Gap, etc.

garden boy. Not a gardener, but a small boy employed to water plants etc.

gatedoor. See COMPOUND REDUNDANT.

gaudeamus, (now obsolete), "a college students' merrymaking", S.O.E.D., was a term applied to a spree, whose two main attractions were black-pudding-and-souse and rum, which used to take place in the Scotland District.

gear down. *Charles was all geared down for the party!* i.e dressed up to the nines, elaborately dressed.

gen. Past tense of give: *He gen him the money.*

georgie bundle. A bundle made up of various oddments. Georgie bundles are plentiful when families are moving.

get. The past tense of the verb is used impersonally instead of "there is" or "there are", as, *They got a big pond on the estate.* Get **away**: to come to words, to quarrel, as, *The two of them always getting away about some trifle or other.* Get **by**: to fare ill or well as the case may be, as, *Well, how did you get by at the interview?* Get **on**: to behave in an unseemly manner, as, *Just because you can't have your own way, look how you getting on!*

gittima. (Phonetic). This word, recently brought to my attention, had best perhaps be illustrated by the following dialogue:
Jones: That's a nice engine on your boat. What make is it?
Smith: Well, it's really a gittima, you see.
Jones: What's that? Japanese?
Smith: No, silly, a gi'-to-me...a gift.

give out. A housewife always gives out the dinner, i.e. instructs the cook what the menu is to be.

glassbottle, grassbottle. Broken glass, especially bits of broken bottles. The tops of walls were formerly provided with glass bottle to keep out intruders, and the word seems to have been once recognised as good English: *cf. Still is that fur as soft as when the lists In youth thou enter'dst on glass-bottl'd wall. (Keats: Sonnet to a Cat.)*

go. The following idioms may be noted: (i) *Go away!* Get along with you, I don't believe you; (ii) *Is there anything to go by?* may be translated as Is there any rum to hand? (iii) *He gone 'cross* (across), It's all up with him; (iv) *Those two batsmen gone down, boy.* Those two batsmen are well set; *John gone down in the peas and rice,* John is eating the peas and rice ravenously; (v) *Friday gone,* last Friday; *Friday gone week,* a week ago last Friday. See **coming**. The phrase, **I gone**, is frequently used instead of good-bye.

goanna. From *Usage and Abusage (Eric Partridge):* "Goanna is popularly used in Australia for the monitor lizards (Varanidae): it is a corruption of the word iguana, though the true *iguana* is not found in that country." For the word "Australia", substitute "Barbados".

goat. Goat **knee:** a little known term applied to the callous sometimes formed, as the result of carrying heavy loads, on the top of the head, the callous having the appearance of the horny skin of a goat's knee. Goat **pills,** not inappropriately, goats' droppings. Goat **mouth:** to say that someone has a goat mouth is to imply that the person is reputed to bring ill luck to or blight any plan with which he says he does not agree. See also **put one's mouth on.**

goat heaven. A state of bliss. *And when she looked at me and smiled, I tell you I was in goat heaven!* Why the goat, of all animals, should have been singled out by Barbadians to typify such a state is obscure. Also **kiddy kingdom.**

goat-money. Used to refer to a fairly large collection of small coins, so that a person paying a debt in silver and copper might say *Sorry I got to pay you in all this goat-money.* A possible explanation is that it may be used contemptuously with reference to **goat pills.**

gobble. (Noun). Gob of spittle.

goblet. The earthenware vessels in which water is kept to make it cool are really *goglets* or *gugglets* (C.O.D.) but goblet (metal or glass drinking-cup) perhaps sounds more refined.

godhorse. A stick-insect of the family Phasmidae.

God spare life. The B'adian version of *deo volente,* as, *I'll see you tomorrow, God spare life.*

go-forwards. Sandals that have no heel strap; in such foot-wear it is obviously difficult to step backwards.

goggle. Probably from "guggle," 1680. (Slang) The windpipe, S.O.E.D. The Adam's apple. An unusually large one is known as a rum goggle.

good. (i) As an adverb of manner implying a higher degree of excellence than the grammatical **well.** *He writes well* is half-hearted praise; *He writes good,* unstinted. (ii) As an adverb of degree: extremely. Hence the expression *He good bad* which equals the accepted colloquialism *pretty ugly* in absurdity. (iii) As a noun: (a) news; as, *Well, old man, what's all the good?* (b) An I.O.U. a document good for the amount in question; *He gave me a good for the money I lent him.* (iv) As an adjective in the expression *good for oneself,* which means accountable to no one for one's actions, especially if these be of a loose or immoral nature; as *You needn't think she going pay any attention to what you say; she good for sheself.* (v) see **hair.**

good night. A phrase used to express greetings at night as well as at parting.

grabble, although no longer current Standard English, is listed in the S.O.E.D., as "To seize 1796", a meaning which it still retains locally, generally along with the word, hold, as, *Before he knew what was happening, the policeman grabbled hold of him.*

grabbler. A metal implement used by market vendors in digging potatoes and yams in the plantation fields.

grain. (i) Peas or beans. *How you selling your grain?* (ii) A fish-spear or harpoon. The word is now obsolete in Standard English (S.O.E.D.) being replaced by *grains,* originally the plural of the word. Grain is also used as a verb: *The fisherman grained the conger.*

grass piece. See **piece.**

great-kind. Applied chiefly to pure-bred stock, poultry especially, and also sometimes to fruit or vegetables of best quality. *But look how she walking 'long the road, though! Just like a great-kind pigeon.*

Green, The. The area surrounding the Nelson statute at the eastern approach to Broad Street; also known as Trafalgar Square. "The Green took its name from the sward adjoining Captain Jeremiah Eggington's house, commonly known as Eggington's Green, and later as 'the Green'. Here at one time stood the pillory and stocks where offenders were punished. There was also a horse pond in which a ducking-stool was placed for the punishment of women declared to be 'common scolds'." The Barbados Advocate 5th December, 1950, Letter of E.M. Shilstone. (*Journal of the B.H.M.S. Vol. XVIII, Nos. 12*) At the western extremity of Broad Street is the Lower Green.

grind ginger. An expressive phrase, though not very common, to denote working oneself into a temper, as, *You better not trouble Mummy now, boy: like she grindin' ginger.*

green pea. The shell of a small limpet, Patella occidentalis, which is common on the rocks along the shore. This little green shell, much smaller than the pea after which it is named, is used in the making of brooches and other ornaments.

grey goose. A term applied to a mulatto of fair complexion, with greenish-grey eyes and gingery hair that is almost the same colour as his skin.

grief lump. Constriction of the throat occasioned by emotional distress.

grig. Used exactly in the same sense as **grain.**

grogoon. (Facetious.) A word applied to well-seasoned old topers.

ground. Often used to refer to the floor of a house, or even of a car or other conveyance, as *Don't put it on the seat* (of the car); *put it on the ground.* Found in the following compounds: (i) ground **apples:** stones; (ii) ground **provisions:** applied to potatoes, yams, eddoes, etc. The compound is not listed in either the S.O.E.D. or the C.O.D.

grounder. (Cricket) A shooter.

groundsel. The S.O.E.D. states "A timber serving as a foundation to carry a superstructure esp. a wooden building; the lowest of a wooden frame work; a ground-plate; hence, the foundation of any structure. Now chiefly *techn.*" The groundsel of the Barbadian chattel house is the foundation of stones, generally without mortar, on which the groundplates are supported.

grumpus-back. A surly person. The significance of grumpus is obvious, but why *back?*

guard wall. A low wall erected at dangerous curves and corners of the highway. Not listed in either the S.O.E.D. or the C.O.D.

gudgeon. The phrase "Gilman mill gudgeon" used to be employed in the following simile: *You mout' hard as Gilman mill gudgeon.* Enquiries as to who Mr. Gilman was or where his mill was situated have met with no response.

guineaman. A species of flying-fish almost twice as large as the common variety. Sometimes called *flying fish father.*

gun-mout's. (Slang). In the hey-day of the "Oxford bags", those who preferred to continue wearing the tight-fitting, narrow-hemmed trousers were frequently subjected to ridicule; the trousers were said to resemble gun-barrels or gunmout(h)s, and street urchins would exclaim "buddung" or "biddim" derisively at every opportunity, such exclamations being imitative of the report of a gun.

guttaperc. The old-fashioned name for a catapult.

gypsy. (Adjective). Always used in the sense of meddlesome, officious. *Why don't you mind you own business? You too damn gypsy.*

H.

Habra, Dabra and the crew. Tom, Dick and Harry.

hadja-buck. An uncouth, ill-bred person.

had not. Elliptical form of "had it not been for" and often used to introduce a conditional clause in the negative; as, *Had not he was sick, he would have parade on them.*

hag. (Verb.) To worry, harass or pester: *These children hagging me out.* Hence, as a noun, to apply to persons (male or female) who are considered nuisances. The sign *No Hags Allowed* is often displayed on lorries. A **bicycle** hag: one who is always borrowing someone else's cycle; a **picture** hag; one whose chief enjoyment is going to the cinema; a **sailor** hag; a girl who prefers to go around with visiting sailors than with Barbadian young men.

hail. To hail for; to back a team enthusiastically and, most often, vociferously, as, *He hails for Pickwick.* Hence, **hailer,** one who hails for a team.

hair. The hair of the head is referred to as being either **good** or **bad.** The terms denote the distinction between that of the Negro and of the other races. Hair-**drizzle:** a very fine drizzle. Hair-**ball:** a hard, compact ball of hair sometimes found in the stomachs of cattle.

half-bottle, halfie. A small bottle (3 gills) of rum.

half-hearty, not to be confused with half-hearted, denotes a condition of health that is neither good nor bad, and is generally employed when the person has not wholly recovered from some illness, as, in reply to a query as to the person's health, *Half-hearty. I had a bad cold in the bowels all last week.*

hand. (i) The entire arm: *He got his hand broken just above the elbow.* (See **foot.**) (ii) cluster of bananas growing from a central stem and resembling a bunch of green fingers. (iii) A knock at cricket: *Do I get a hand this afternoon?* (iv) The phrase *a good writing hand* (hand-writing) may be noted.

happy days. A slang term for the breadfruit.

hard. In compounds: (i) hard-back: (a) the black beetle, (b) (Adjective.) *Fancy an old hard back man like you saying a thing like that!* (Cf. hardened sinner.); (ii) hard-**ears**, or hard-**eared;** disobedient; (iii) hard-**mouth:** employed in the same sense.

hare-rabbit. A hare. (See **COMPOUND REDUNDANT**).

have. To have **in**: to contain. *This cake has in currants;* and not this cake has currents in it. **They** have: sometimes used impersonally (see get) as *They have bus stops all along the route.*

head. (Verb). To carry a load on the head, as, *The women were heading the canes to the cart.*

headtie. (Noun.) The style in which the kerchief is worn to cover the head. The old-fashioned head-tie made of a large white kerchief is fast disappearing, though it is still favoured by some agricultural labourers.

hear. (i) Used intransitively, obey, as *Child, why you won't hear?* Also, often with preposition to, as, *He won't hear to me.* (ii) Often used as an injunction at the end of a sentence, as *I'll see you tomorrow, hear!* (iii) The well-known Hear, hear! is often rendered, sometimes facetiously, as Hear **you!** or Hear **thee!** (iv) The expression, hear the **shout,** or, hear the **hurrah,** may be noted.: *When you hear the shout you'll find out he was the thief,* i.e. when you get to the truth of the matter.

Heart affection. A heart condition. The heart is affected.

heat cloud. Heavy, low-hanging cloud frequent during the months of August and September usually, and portending heat.

heavy-bread. A loaf of bread containing neither baking-powder nor soda, usually containing chipped coconut. Sometimes known as a *coconut bread.*

height. (i) *He wouldn't take my height*: He wouldn't even notice me. Perhaps, because he wouldn't as much as raise his eyes to meet those of the speaker. (ii) *He made height down the road:* He ran at full speed down the road. Perhaps a metaphor taken from the flight of birds (iii) The phrase **lower** your height is often used instead of stoop or bend.

hef(t). "Dial. and U.S. ... to lift to judge the weight." S.O.E.D. *Hef' this and tell me if it don't weigh more than two pounds.*

hellion. A wild, devil-may-care fellow.

hi, to be noted in combination with *gee* and *whoa,* as, *I don't know what to say to him: he won't hi, gee, nor whoa,* i.e. he'll neither start, move on, nor stop: it's impossible to get him to do anything.

Hickey, The. An imaginary country district into which good manners and genteel customs have never penetrated, as *Boy, you ain't got no manners? Where you come from? The Hickey?* C.f. country hick (U.S.)

hide. (Cricket). *Bowl at the man; don't hide the ball* is an injunction often heard when the bowler is adopting modern negative tactics.

hind claw. *If I lose my job, I have no hind claw like you, you know.* A very expressive way of referring to some means of financial support other than one's recognised means of income.

hog. Found in the following compounds: (i) hog-**cow:** the water buffalo, a few of which were once imported; (ii) hog-**food:** hog-wash; (iii) hog-**thomas:** an uncouth, ill-mannered person.

hog up. To speak roughly or discourteously to some one, as *The lawyer hog up the witness when he find out he was telling lies.*

hold strain. A recent popular phrase which is equivalent to 'take it easy', or the once familiar 'don't tear your shirt'.

hole. (i) The area, varying from 5 to 6 square feet in which sugar cane, corn, or ground provisions are planted. (ii) The produce obtained from a single planting in such an area. Very often potatoes, yams, etc. are sold by the hole. **Marl-hole:** a quarry from which limestone marl is obtained; **white-hole:** a bathing pool made by removing the large stones from the coral reef. Also **white-pool.**

hoose. To bowl at great speed. *He was hoosing it down.* An echo word. Whiz?

hoot. To make one hoot: to cause grave discomfort, inconvenience or pain to one; as, *The mosquitoes made me hoot last night.*

hop-and-drop. *He walks hop-and-drop;* he walks with a pronounced limp.

hopping-ball. A tennis ball.

horn. ·(Verb.) To cuckold, or to supplant a rival. It is interesting to note that this word which played such an all-important part in the Elizabethan playwright's vocabulary should still linger on in the island. A correspondent mentions she heard quite a small boy say to his sweetheart who had been flirting with another youngster "So you horning me then!"

horse. Horse-**eye:** the horse-mackerel or cavally. Horse-**nicker:** the seeds of the tree "Caesalpina bonducella which are hard and grey about the size of a hazel nut, are roasted, ground, and then prepared like coffee. The resulting extract is given to patients with oedema, both cardiac and renal." (*Iris Bayley: B.H.M.S. Vol. XVI, No. 3).* Horse **up:** (Slang.) (i) To vent one's displeasure as, *When we told him what we had done, he horsed up on us. (ii)* To dance in the modern manner; *as, I saw you horsing up at the club last night.*

horstilish. A corruption of 'hostile'. Cf. 'horspital for the intrusion of the letter 'r'.'

hot sauce, a bottle of which, I suppose, is to be found in almost every Barbadian home, is classified by Mrs. Gladys Skinner in her *A Souvenir of Barbados* as a "minor industry" of the island. "Hot sauce is a mixture of peppers, vinegar, and mustard, with the addition of onions, tumeric and perhaps other herbs according to taste. It is eaten as a relish in soups or with other foods (ibid)."

hot toddy. A cure for a cold. It was the water in which a burnt corn or loaf of bread was soaked. Rum was added and the mixture drunk hot. It is interesting to note, however, that the word, hot, in the phrase *a hot drink,* does not refer to temperature but to alcoholic content.

house-cart. A trailer formerly used to move chattel houses.

house-clear. I heard this compound for the first time quite recently. I had enquired after the health of a very old woman whom I hadn't seen for some time and her son replied *She much better now her face fill out, and she walking about, but she can't get out, so she is a little house-clear.* That is to say, a little pale from lack of sunlight.

house spot. A spot of land upon which a house is built "...in Barbados ... a man's most treasured ambition (is) to own a 'house spot'." T. S. Simey: *Welfare and Planning in the West Indies.*

hout, howt. Archaic form of hoot, "drive (person) out, away, &c. by hooting". But the local form of the word implies a driving away by any sign of disapproval, as *His aunt used to treat him bad and hout him like a dog.* Probably, too, echoic, "Get out!"

how-dee. How d'ye do. *Tell she how-dee 'nough 'nough hear?* Be sure to give her my best regards.

huckum, hukkum. How come? Why?

humbug. There is no notion of fraud or imposture connected with the local use of the word; to humbug is to annoy; a humbug is a nuisance.

hurricane months. The old saying
> June, too soon;
> July, stand by;
> August, you must;
> September, remember
> October, all over.

is one that is not likely to be soon forgotten.

hush. The colloquial Shut up! is generally rendered by *Hush your mouth!*

hymeneal. An invitation to a wedding printed on satin. It must always be returned accompanied with a gift, since it has to serve many persons. (*Harrisonian, July 1926.*) See also **compliment.**

I.

ignorant. In addition to its proper use, the word is frequently employed to denote some action which may be either rash or carefree, as, *Boy, stop aggravating me before I go and do something ignorant,* or, *Man, play ignorant and score the runs fast.*

imphee. "A species of wild sugar cane, Holchus sacchaatus, also called African or Chinese Sugar cane, Broom Corn Sorgho, and Planter's Friend 1857": S.O.E.D. Formerly used as a fodder, but now rarely cultivated. The word is not listed in the C.O.D.

indifferent. In its sense of "unconcerned, apathetic, insensible", the word has come to be used chiefly as a term of abuse, connoting worthless, or good-for-nothing, as, *But there's a long, indifferent, lazy man!*

ink fish. A name applied to the squid and cuttlefish.

interval. A cart path between cultivated fields. *The watchman strolled down the interval.* "An open space lying between two things or two parts of one thing; a gap, an opening 1489," states the S.O.E.D.

itch. Frequently used instead of 'scratch', as, *Itch my back for me, please.*

J.

Jack. Used in some country districts as a familiar nominative of address, as, *Hey, Jack, you hear what happen this morning?*

Jackson fowl-roost. The phrase *in Jackson fowl-roost* signifies being in trouble. Origin unknown.

jack-spaniard. The wild-bee or wasp.

Janet. The hurricane of September 1955.

Jenkins. *He gone down to Jenkins:* He has been taken to the Mental Hospital.

jessamine. Sometimes used to refer to the frangipani tree or blossom.

Jo and Johnny. A dance which used to be performed by labourers on the sugar plantations at **crop-over** (Harvest home).

Joe Clarke. The squawk of the guinea-bird is represented by the cry *Joe Clarke, Joe Clarke, come back, come back!*

John Bayley guts. Originally cane syrup boiled to a toffee-like consistency and now applied to any preserves prepared from fruit which has been boiled to too high a pitch. The sweetmeat owes its name to John Bayley, (circ, 1820), its originator. Also known, by association of ideas, as John **Belly** guts.

jook. (Verb and noun.) To stick or punch with some pointed object; a wound or blow so received. *Ma, Charlie jook me in the eye with his finger. The Carpenter got a bad nail-jook.* Hence used metaphorically, as, *I got jooked in the eye that time,* i.e, I got properly tricked on that occasion. The following definition from *Webster's New Collegiate Dictionary, 2nd Edition* may prove interesting: **"juke, jook, joint.** (Apparently of West African origin.) Orig. Southern U.S. Originally an out of the way shack used by Negro turpentine workers as a drinking and dancing resort; hence any roadhouse or dance hall or like resort for drinking or dancing especially to the music of an automatic player of phonograph records that plays one record on deposit of a coin in the slot, called a juke-box or juke". It is interesting to note the origin of the juke, but why were the shacks originally called jukes or jooks? Because their patrons were "jooked in the eye"? Yet another suggestion: the S.O.E.D. lists "jut, sb. Obs. or dial. 1553. A push, thrust or shove against a resting body; the shock of collision. Verb obs. or dial. 1548 (app. onomatopoeic) i. intr. To strike, knock or push against something – 1628. ii trans. To push, thrust, shove, jolt, to knock against something 1565." Jooking-**board,** washboard.

jug, jug-jug. A famous Christmas dish. From the *Barbados Gift Book:* (Ingredients: 8 pints peas, 3/4 lb. salt beef, 3/4lb. salt pork, 1/4 lb. butter. 1 bunch of green seasoning cut up very fine). Boil peas and meat until cooked. Pass through a mincer and pound until smooth. Put 1/2 pint of stock from peas to cook with seasoning 5 minutes, then add your guinea corn, stirring quickly for 10 minutes. Add rest of ingredients and cook slowly for 20 minutes. Put in butter before serving.

jump up. The spirit of carnival recently introduced into the ball room has led to that form of dancing known as jumping up, which is precisely what the words imply.

jury road. Road provided by a court as access to Land otherwise inaccessible.

justly. Exactly. *I can't justly say where he lives.* Also English dialect.

just-now. Not to be confused with just now, meaning immediately. Just-now means a few moments ago. *I'll attend to the matter just now,* but *I saw him walking down the street just-now.*

K.

keep. No Barbadian makes a noise, he keeps it. *Stop keeping that noise, will you?* is to be heard at any time, any day, in any school. Probably an Elizabethan heritage: cf. Maria's *What a caterwauling do you keep here? – Twelfth Night, Act II, Sc. 3.* Also the colloquial *keep quiet.*

keep-miss. Kept-woman.

kem. Some action or statement whose intent it is to deceive: as, *When he left he walked down the road, but that was only a kem; I knew he was going next door at Irene.*

kerchief. Although listed in the C.O.D. as "(poet.) handkerchief" has no poetic association whatever locally, but is employed as a shorter form of the word.

kernel. An enlarged gland in the groin. "Now dialect". S.O.E.D.

kiddy kingdom. See **goat heaven.**

kill-cow. "Obsolete except in dialect. 1581. A bully, braggadocio,..." states the S.O.E.D. Occasionally heard in Barbados in this sense, as, *You think you is any kill-cow 'bout here?*

kimboes. *He had his arms in the kimboes:* his arms were akimbo.

kiss. *If I'd known that, I would have hit him, be kiss!* ... Most likely a euphemism for "by Christ".

kneadiness. Morbidly frequent but unaccomplished desire to evacuate the bowels, perhaps due to the sensation of the bowels being kneaded or massaged. Or is the word **neediness,** a euphemism expressing a physical need?

knock. To knock **around.** To hang around, to frequent. To-knock **dog**: to be abundant, as, *fish was knocking dog in the market yesterday.*

knocker. The large, greyish cockroach (Blabera gigantea), so called because it produces a sound of knocking by vibrating its abdomen against wooden partitions. Seldom found in private homes, it would seem to frequent warehouses and very old buildings. Listed in the S.O.E.D. as the *drummer.* Its unpleasant smell is proverbial.

knuck, knucka. Probably derived from knuckle. A *knucka foot* might signify a deformed leg (see *foot*), or leg the foot of which has been amputated.

L.

lady. Frequently used with reference to hawkers, as, *The lady with the tomatoes at the door.*

lag. (Verb). To split a spinning top by launching another spinning top at it.

lame. Usually implying an injury to the foot or leg, this word is frequently used to qualify the word *hand* (arm) in like sense.

landship. A sort of friendly society which frequently holds organised parades of its members all dressed in naval uniform. The landship societies seem to have enjoyed brief periods of intense activity separated by long periods of comparative dormancy. From the middle, and probably earlier, years of the last century, the white-uniformed, gold-tasselled parades have been a familiar sight.

The following extracts from George Bernard's *Wayside Sketches*, should prove interesting: "The Barbados Landship Association boasts of a fleet of over thirty 'ships' ... The landship is usually a small house on the top of which are two poles supporting what is obviously intended to be a wireless aerial... Strict naval decorum (is) observed ... Visits between the various units are of frequent occurrence... When the combined ships 'cruise the high seas' the band leads the way, followed by the Lord High Admiral ... closely attended by his A.D.C. and bodyguard composed of the officers of the fleet: Sea Lords, Fleet Admiral, Vice-Admiral of Combine, Rear-Admiral of Combine, Fleet Admiral, etc. The various ships then follow on, officers in the van, followed by petty officers ... then by the Stars (or nurses) each of whom has a pair of scissors suspended from her waist". Many years have elapsed since *Wayside Sketches* was published and "a cruise of combined ships' has not been seen for some time.

land-turtle. The tortoise.

'larmer. An alarmist. *Don't mind he. He is a regular old 'larmer.*

lash. (Noun). Properly stroke with thong, whip, etc., but used to mean a blow with any object, as, *He let go a lash at me with his stick.* Hence, **stick**-lash.

lated. This form of belated is still in use, as, *Excuse me, but the rain had me lated.* Cf. "Now spurs the lated traveller apace..." *Macbeth III, 3.*

lay by. *I'll see you when school lay by;* i.e. I'll see you after school this evening.

L chamber. See **Ell-Chamber.**

lazaretto dog dead in St. Philip. This quaint expression implies that some philandering husband has met his death while visiting his lady love far from home.

lead. A lead pencil. *Lend me your lead;* or, *He uses a blue lead for corrections.*

leader boy. A boy who used to run beside, and sometimes ride, the leading mule of a team drawing a cart with produce from the sugar plantations.

leather bat. A bat; the epithet being used to distinguish it from "bats" or moths.

leave. A Barbadian seldom if ever misses a bus: the bus always leaves him. *I was so busy shopping that the bus left me.*

lend. Perhaps from the Barbadian's extreme reluctance to part with anything, he seldom speaks of "giving anyone hell": *"Boy, if those fellows interfere with us, we going to lend them hell."*

let 'lone. To leave alone. Also used as substantive, as, *You better make a let 'lone* i.e., You'd best not worry.

liard. (Adjective.) Possessing the reputation of a liar, as, *Nobody going believe you: you too liard.*

lick. (Verb) In addition to the many currently accepted slang phrases found in the C.O.D., as "thrash (person, fault out of a person); hasten, surpass comprehension;" the following local varieties are interesting: lick **(a)bout**, to live a careless, loose life, as, *After he done licking 'bout, he going expect any decent woman to marry him!;* lick **(a)way**, to knock something away, as, *He lick 'way the ball in the canes;* lick **cork**, a sort of rough and ready game played in shallow water near the shore, the players somersaulting and splashing one another; hence, metaphorically, to enjoy oneself in a somewhat rowdy manner, as, *Boy, we licked cork at the party last night;* lick **down,** to knock down, as, *The cyclist licked him down;* lick **out,** to waste or spend extravagantly, as, *He'll soon lick out all his money;* lick **up,** to destroy completely, as, *He lick up the car 'gainst the wall.* The idiomatic *Da' fo' lick you* (That for lick you) may also be noted. Well-nigh untranslatable, its tenor is, To blazes with you. (Noun). (i) Girl friend or paramour, as, *She is my lick* ; (ii) used in the plural, a thrashing, as, *I used to get lots of licks at school.* Hence to **line** in licks, to thrash thoroughly.

lickerish, liquorish. Often imagined to be peculiarly Barbadian but listed in the C.O.D. with precisely the same shades of meaning with which it is used locally.

lick mouth. "A popular dispenser of local gossip. One who kisses and tells." Louis Lynch: *The Barbados Book.*

lift. The layers of a large cake are popularly known as lifts. *Those two boys eat up the whole of the top lift of the wedding cake.*

like. Used elliptically to mean *It looks like ...,* as, *Like you like music,* or, *this boy like he can play cricket.*

limbless. A very expressive word: bereft of the use of one's limbs, temporarily paralysed by shock, as, *When I hear 'bout poor Joe, the news had me limbless.*

lime. (Verb.) To stand in a group on a side-walk or near some frequented spot, and indulge in chit-chat, sometimes passing remarks at passers-by, especially females; to loiter in groups. Perhaps the following passage from one of Samuel Selvon's short stories may illustrate its use: "Brackley settle down ... in Ladbroke Grove with easy communications for liming out in the evening after work ... he would meet the boys and they would lime by the Arch ... and keep a weather eye open forwhatever might appear..." Also **pick** a lime.

limeskin. (Slang). A felt hat that has seen its best days.

ling. In any game of marbles the ring is always called the ling.

lining. Used by laundresses to denote a woman's slip or petticoat.

lining cold. Properly, lying-in: a cold caught by a mother soon after childbirth.

lion fish. The sculpin.

liquor. Frequently in its older sense of "liquid product", especially of the sugar cane. The juice before boiling is known as **raw** liquor, after its preliminary boiling as **cracked**, or **crack** liquor; after further boiling to the stage before crystallisation is reached as **sweet** liquor.

62

Little England. "Barbadians love to call their island 'little England' ", writes the Barbadian poet M. J. Chapman, in the notes to his *Barbados and other Poems* as long ago as 1835.

load. Often used figuratively to denote a great deal, as, *Boy you going get a load o' licks when your father find out.*

loblolly. When these notes were being compiled, a friend of mine mentioned it to me as a memory of his childhood: his nurse used to refer to biscuits broken up in gravy as "loblolly sauce". But as no one else had ever heard of the word, we concluded that it was a happy invention of his nurse. A few days ago he informed me he had actually come upon the word in the following context: Rabelais' *Gargantua and Pantagruel,* Book IV, Ch. XL: "Mondam, that first invented Madam's sauce and for that discovery, was thus called in the Scoth-French dialect – Loblolly, Slabber-chops, ...", etc. As the translation of Book IV was first published in English in 1694, loblolly sauce would seem to have had a long history; it would be interesting to know whether any of our readers are acquainted with it. As these notes go to print Mr. E.M. Shilstone writes: "The early settlers introduced the word. In reference to the various kinds of food which he found in use, Ligon mentions *mayes* (i.e. indian corn) and says, p. 31, "we have a way of feeding our christian servants with this *mayes* which is by pounding it in a large mortar and boiling it in water to the thickness of frumenty; and so put in a tray such a quantity as will serve a mess of seven or eight people, give it to them cold, and scarce afford them salt with it. This we call *lob-lollie.* But the negroes when they come to be fed with this are much discounted, and cry out, O, O, no more lob-lob!' "

local. Sometimes used with reference to a person or thing of no account.

looard, loward. Colloquial form of leeward.

look. *Look me here* is a far more usual statement than "Here I am".

look for. Two idiomatic uses of this phrase may be noted: (i) to pay a friendly visit on someone, as, *We went to look for Aunt Mary last Sunday;* and (ii) to indicate the likelihood of a shower, as *Best not go out now; it looking for rain.*

lose out. One loses money and other possessions, but plans, schemes, etc., are always lost out; as *He try to get me fire from the job, but he lose out bad.*

loss occurs in the phrase "loss 'way" which conveys the following meanings: (i) to be lost among something, or to fade out, as *The ball loss 'way 'mong the canes,* or, *The stars loss 'way behind the trees;* hence, metaphorically, *After all those years in the business, it looks like he loss 'way,* i.e., he has failed to obtain recognition for his service; (ii) to denote loss of flesh or weight, as *Since she sick she loss 'way a lot. O loss!* O lawks, O Lord.

loud-mouth. An epithet conferred on noisy, quarrelsome, or otherwise stentorian-voiced persons. *You mean to tell me you don't know that loud-mout' woman that does live up the lane?*

low-rate. To belittle.

low(er)side. To the leeward or west. See also **above, below,** and **upperside.**

M.

madam. Often used with reference to hucksters or fruit-sellers from the Windward Islands especially St. Lucia, because in former days many of them wore the native creole dress. The plural of the word is *madams. A lot of madams live in Nelson Street.* Also frequently used to refer to the mistress of a household, as, *The madam tell me I can cook good.*

mad staggers. Classified in the C.O.D. as "blind staggers: kinds of disease of brain and spinal cord esp. in horses and cattle; giddiness."

magasse. Variant of *bagasse.*

main-guard. Law breakers are usually *carried to the main-guard,* i.e., to the central police station. The S.O.E.D. states under this word "1653 ... the keep of a castle; also the building within a fortress in which the 'main-guard' (a guard having the custody of all disturbers of the peace, drunkards, etc. 1706) is lodged."

make. *She is making a child:* She is pregnant. Make **out,** to fare; as, *Well, how did you make out in the exam?;* make **up,** (i) to man-handle; as, *The policeman had him made up by the seat of his pants;* (ii) to contort (one's face), grimace, as, *He made up his face at me;* make someone **come 'round,** to give someone a proper dressing down, as, *The boss made Jones come 'round this morning;* make **sport:** the expression *You making sport!* is often used as a retort to a statement which is regarded as incredible or absurd. **Make** some one **hoot:** see **hoot.** Make **change:** to give money in exchange for coins, notes, etc. of greater value.

MALAPROPISMS. These are many and various; the following, however, may be regarded as common currency: **Bim** (absit omen) a dust bin; **costive** costly; **cupella,** propeller; **human cry,** hue and cry; **portugal,** portico, **refuge,** refuse (noun); **spawn,** span; **spry,** spray; **swivelled,** shrivelled.

malicious. Most frequently used with its "occasional" meaning: "Inclined to tease; mischievous." S.O.E.D. *This little child too malicious!*

man. The favourite nominative of address of the Barbadian. The sex of the person addressed is immaterial, as, *Let's go to the pictures, Mary , man.*

manager. Without qualification, invariably the manager of a sugar **estate. Manager belly,** a paunch.

manjak. A type of asphalt known as Gilsonite, found in a few isolated spots in the "Scotland" district. A detailed account of its properties, etc., is to be found under the heading *The Mineral Resources of Barbados* (R.H. Emtage) in *The Barbados Handbook,* ed. E.G. Sinckler, 1913. *The B.M.H.S. Vol. XXIII No. 1* states: "This is a variety of bitumen and originates from petroleum oxidation.

The occurrence of manjak is connected with the flow of mud volcanoes. Veins of this substance occur in parts of St. Joseph and were formerly mined and used as fuel for sugar furnaces, later being exported for use in the manufacture of paints and varnishes. The mining of manjak was abandoned when synthetic substances were found to be cheaper for the purpose."

Mapp's mill-yard. The simile, *as hot as Mapp's mill-yard,* still lingers on among the older generation. I have not been able to discover its origin.

marish and the parish. *Marish and the parish will be there:* i.e., everybody. Why 'marish' (poet & dial., marshy, such as is produced in a marsh 1513 S.O.E.D.) should be linked with 'parish' is not clear; possibly on account of the rhyming effect.

mark. The phrase *not marking myself,* is a sort of formula used to avert an evil omen, as, *His face was cut open here* (pointing to the spot), *not marking myself* ... Cf. the Nurse's speech:

> I saw the wound, I saw it with mine eyes —
> God save the mark! — here on his manly breast...
> *Romeo and Juliet, Act. III, Sc. 2.*

marl-hole. (See hole.) A quarry from which limestone is obtained.

maroon. (Obsolete.) (i) Picnic; (ii) Pot-luck. *The Harrisonian* July, 1925.

mash. (Verb.) Properly "crush, pound, to pulp" (C.O.D.) is used locally in the sense of *step on,* as, *Don't mash my foot.* In this context it may be noted that the expression *Mash the gas* is current U.S. slang as well. To mash **up**: to break up, destroy; as *He mash up the bicycle.* Mash-**mout'(h):** applied to a sunken or recessive mouth, as *That mash-mout' white lady.*

mashiated. Most likely a happy confusion of words and ideas: emaciated and **mash**. Destroyed, as, *The house was mashiated in the hurricane.*

master. (i) Sometimes used as a title instead of Sir; as, *Master, you* *can tell me the time please?* (ii) Also used of male animals, stallions, rams, etc., hired out for service. *When you sending the goat to the master?*

mattie. *Them two is matties,* i.e., They are bosom-friends. Used only with reference to females; sometimes conveying the suggestion of Lesbianism.

mauby. "...a drink which is sold in the streets, carried on the vendor's head in a can to which a basal spigot is attached. Mauby is made from bark, boiled in water for about an hour, and concentrated to a basic extract. When making the drink, some of the stock is diluted with water; sugar and vanilla essence are added to taste, and a block of ice put into the can, along with the prepared mixture. The result is a bitter-sweet drink, with a frothy head, popular for quenching the thirst, and for "cooling" the blood. In trying to discover the type of bark used, a great many different plants are quoted ... Professor C. Y. Shepherd ... states that the Acting Curator, Forestry Department, British Guiana, says that "mauby bark" is a product of the tree *Gouiania domingensis,*... This plant is also mentioned by Schomburgk, along with two others, *Zizyphus jujuba* and *Ceamothus columbrinus.* The *U.S. Dispensatory* (1947) states that "Mabee" bark is yielded by *Caemothus reclinatus* (L'Herit) or *Columbrina reclinata* (Brongn), and it contains a glycoside. All these plants belong to the order *Rhamnuceae,* and it is probable that they are all used, one being substituted for the other, when not available." *Iris Bayley: The Bush Trees of Barbados: Journal of the B.M.H.S., Vol. XVI, No. 3.*

maulsprigging. A thrashing. Current in U.S.

Maxwell pond. *All his money gone in Maxwell pond* is a saying denoting that someone's money has been lost in some investment.

maypole. The infloresence of the Agave Mexicana. The "poles" attain a height of 20 feet or more, and, as they are buoyant, are used by fishermen when they go diving sea-eggs.

The following lines from M. J. Chapman's *Barbados and other Poems* (1835) give a poet's description of the maypole in bloom:

> Here towering in its pride, the maypole glows
> Whose pointed top a bee-swarmed circlet shows

Of waving yellow; whose high-branched stem
Takes back the rapt thought to Jerusalem
Showing the candlestick that stood of old
In the first temple, chased of purest gold.

mean. *How you mean?* is the more usual way of asking "What do you mean?" but when these words are used as an exclamation, they have quite a different meaning. Thus, should someone be asked if he enjoyed himself at a party, the reply, *How you mean* would imply that the question was almost superfluous: he had had a whale of a time.

meat. Cane-meat or fodder. A statement like *I just gave the horse the meat* is likely to prove disconcerting unless the local use of the word is borne in mind.

meeting. Often, a prayer-meeting. Hence meeting-**house:** a room or hall in which prayer-meetings are held. Also, a private saving scheme among a few persons (say, six), each contributing a sum, usually $10 per month, with one of the number drawing the sum total in turn per month; also called a **turn.**

melts. It will no doubt come as a shock to most Barbadians to learn that that prime delicacy, flying fish melts, should really be flying fish milt, ("The roe or spawn of the male fish; the soft roe of fishes 1483." S.O.E.D.) But the local word, with its verbal association, is certainly more appropriate.

merrywing. Too charming a name to be applied to the midge that frequents some beaches at sundown. Also known as the **sand-fly.**

mice, micey. Frequently used as the singular, mouse.

mile tree. The casuarina.

mill, in compounds: mill-**points,** the arms of a wind-mill to which the sails were attached; the mill-**sails,** canvas attached to the points; mill-**yard,** open yard space surrounding the mill.

mind. *My mind give me not to sell the donkey.* That is to say, I can give no reason for not selling the donkey: I just feel that I shouldn't.

The expressions, *my mind give me,* or *my mind tell me,* are very common. Also, attention, as, *I don't pay no mind to anything he say.* In its sense of "look after, have the care of", the word is found in two local expressions: (i) *minding monkeys,* i.e., keeping an eye on monkeys to prevent their incursions in a field of growing crops; and (ii) at football, the *min'er* (minder), the goalkeeper.

miss. Used as title of both unmarried and married women.

Miss Muggins. I am told that in the windward parishes anyone wearing an article of clothing regarded as demode is asked *Hey, you buy that at Miss Muggins?* Miss Muggins (also Miss **Shekky**) is taken to represent shopkeepers of a former day.

Mistress. The archaic nominative of address has survived in Barbados, and may be heard any day on the lips of any servant or huckster addressing the mistress of the household, as, *I want some more butter, mistress. Mistress, you want any useful limes?*

mob-o-'ton. (Slang.) The meaning is perhaps best illustrated by examples, as, *He is a mob-o-'ton of batsman,* or, *She got a mob-o-'ton of backside.*

mockstick. A figure of ridicule.

molly. Hair coiled and worn "bun" fashion.

molly-booby. (i) Any large moth. (ii) A silly person, a duffer, (at cricket) a "rabbit".

monkey. Properly monkey-pot: "vessel used in tropical countries for containing water, 1897" S.O.E.D. Not listed in the C.O.D. Also used as an adjective, cf. U.S. monkey business, as in such phrases as *monkey motions, monkey faces, monkey man, etc.*

morphy. Hermaphrodite.

moses. A small roughly-constructed dinghy. Mr. Ian Gale writes in the *Barbados Advocate:* "Have you ever wondered why the fishermen call their small row boats "Moses"? Yes, I know, Moses and the bull-rushes and all that sort of thing. That is probably the original idea behind the name but how the name Moses came to Barbados is a round about sort of way. The Moses was a type of boat used on the Thames 'for lighterage around the 17th century. The New Englanders, who traded a great deal with the West Indies, saw the need for boats in the islands for carrying sugar to the ships so they built Moses boats and sold them in the Caribbean. The Moses was usually about 18ft. long and usually of shallow draft and could be shipped easily on top of the lumber the brigs usually carried to the West Indies. Now the original Moses has disappeared but the name remains."

moss. Frequently used to mean sea-weed. See also **sea-moss,** applied to a specific kind of seaweed.

mostly. Usually, generally. *He does mostly wear a khaki shirt.*

mother-in-law. A strip of torn cuticle near the finger-nail.

mother sally. An aunt-sally.

mould. Pronounced *mole;* "Now dialect. The top or dome of the head; also the fontanelle in an infant's head." S.O.E.D.

Mr. Harding. In former days at the annual feast of **crop over,** it was customary to burn a figure of a man which was called Mr. Harding and which represented hard times.

Mrs. Still generally pronounced with Elizabethan flavour: *Mr. and Mistress Jones.*

M-2 (Two). Motor cars are registered M., P., J., etc. to represent the parishes (St. Michael, St. Philip, St. John, etc.) in which they are licensed; so that the expressions M2, P2, J2, etc., are a facetious way of saying that the speaker travelled by his own two legs.

much. (Verb). To make much of, to caress, or fondle; as *My mother never muches me,* or, *She was muching the kitten.*

munnion. This, the archaic form of *mullion,* is applied to the central, perpendicular, removeable bar to which large doors (especially those in warehouses, etc.,) are bolted for support and security. The form, **munton,** is also used.

must. The barbarisms "must be can" and "must be could" are common: *You must be can understand English,* i.e., You ought certainly to be able to understand English.

muster. Money is usually mustered, not saved or put by, for some specific purpose, as, *He can't muster enough money to pay the rent.*

N.

Nancy story. A corruption of Anancy story. Anancy, the spider like Brer Rabbit, hero of many of the folktales of West Africa which were brought to the West Indies. In Barbados, the nancy story is synonymous with the fairy tale.

nasty. (verb). To make nasty; most commonly used with the intensive *up*, as, *Don't nasty up your clothes, child.*

Nebruary morning. *You can look for he to pay you back Nebruary morning;* i.e., never.

Ned. Some twenty or thirty years ago references to Ned were common. Someone might remark, half-jocularly, *Wulloss, I can't work any more. Ned got me.* Or at cricket voices might be heard from the crowd call out to a fast bowler who had lost his sting, *Take him off! Ned got him.* Who Ned was is not known, but his name stood for lack of proper nourishment, in short, starvation; but the poor Barbadian, too proud to acknowledge such a plight, preferred to introduce the euphemistic Ned.

neediness. See **kneadiness.**

needler. (Obsolete.) Sempstress. *The Harrisonian, July 1925.*

neither. (see **either.**) *I ain't got either wife.* (I haven't a wife), might be rendered by either *I got neither wife,* or, more emphatically, *I ain't got neither wife.* Neither **one** is preferred to the pronoun neither. And there is also the remarkable compound neither-nother (no other), as, *I ain't got neither-nother sixpence.*

Nepsha and Kiah. Tom, Dick, and Harry. Origin unknown.

nerves. Occasionally used in its now obsolete sense of sinews or tendons. Thus, a boy flexing his arms may display his "nerves."

new brand is almost always preferred to brand new.

new sick. Applied to some virulent types of influenza.

next. Frequently used to mean other, when speaking of two objects, as, *Show me your next hand.*

nick. (Slang.) To throw dice.

nigger ten. "A St. Andrew's cross chalked or marked near the spot where an accident or deed of violence took place. It warns people to shun the spot which may be haunted. The sign may conceivably represent the figure of a man stretched on the ground." *Harrisonian.* Also applied to the mark or X made by an illiterate person. An X cut in stone to denote a boundary mark.

nigh. Still used colloquially, as, *The car nigh knocked him down,* or,*We live nigh to you cousin.*

nimbles. (Noun). Fowl-lice.

'nint. (Pronounced to rhyme with pint). Anoint. The procedure of anointing is, in the minds of most of us, associated with some religious ceremony or consecration: not so with the Ba'dian peasant who, seeking speedy relief from colds, sprains, rheumatic pains, or any other form of **bad feels** will *'nint himself* or *get himself 'ninted* with anything from the latest panacea of the patent medicine market to the humbler remedies of shark oil or candle grease.

nit. The Sandpiper. A regular migrant to Barbados, and defined in *The Harrisonian* as "the last resource of the disappointed sportsman."

nothing. (Slang). Used as an adjective to mean *of no consequence,* as *a nothing man,* or, *nothing bowling.*

'nough (enough) connotes rather more in quantity than is, conveyed by the word *enough,* and may be translated as *plenty. Boy, 'nough fish in the market today!*

72

nuh. This sound, rendered phonetically, perhaps a combination of *no* and *eh,* would seem to be peculiarly Barbadian. Its meaning may be gathered from the following examples: *Gimme piece more bread nuh?* (Won't you?); *I can do it to-morrow, nuh?* (Can't I!?); and sometimes repeated, *Nuh? Nuh?* to an unanswered question.

nuse. It is difficult to understand why this word should have acquired the initial "n", for no other word beginning with "u" has been similarly affected. But many thousands of Barbadians refuse to "nuse" the correct form of the word. And who has not heard the familiar street cry, *Get your nuseful limes!* Why the lime, of all commodities, should have been singled out for its especial "nusefulness" is another matter awaiting explanation.

nyam. Eat. Like **unnah** and **warri,** this would appear to be one of the few purely African survivals: even this has been corrupted into **yam.**

O.

oar. (Obsolete in Standard English). Row.

obsocky. *But she look obsocky with she hair do up like that, eh!* That is, outmoded, odd, or otherwise conspicuous, and thus provocative of ridicule.

obstruct' cold. "This does make some obstruction in the blood, this cross-gartering," states Malvolio; and it is interesting to note that Leslie Hotson, in his *The First Night of Twelfth Night,* writes: "Though its sense of a 'blocking' or 'stopping up' had begun to spread to other subjects, *obstruction's* main connotation was still a pathological one." When it is borne in mind therefore that almost any complaint can be classified as a **cold,** and the many Elizabethan archaisms in common speech, it may not be surprising to note that the first indication of pregnancy is frequently attributed to nothing more than an obstruct' cold.

ockya. (Phonetically spelt.) A stick used in the art of **stick-licking** or **science.** The ockya is so called because it is made from a wood of that name. *Schomburgk* (p. 598): *Catalogue of Plants: "The*

Cambooge Trees. No. 347. Calophyllum Calaba, Santa Maria or Calaba Tree. *Bois Marie, Baume Vert, Ocjue,* (Span.)"

odd cent. The term "odd change" or "the odd penny" is common English idiom, but for some unexplained reason the Barbados cent is usually referred to as odd, as, *I haven't got an odd cent in my purse.*

offa (off of), is preferred to the preposition, off; as, *He hit two sixes offa the fast bowler.*

okra, okro is the recognised spelling of the word (S.O.E.D. "1707 apparently West African"), but for some reason or other the spelling "ochroe" has become popular. The okra plant or its pods are known as gumbo in the U.S.

old-time. "Of, belonging to, or characteristic of the olden time," S.O.E.D., is no longer regarded as modern Standard English. Also, **old-timish,** as, *She too old-timish in she ways.*

Old Year's night always; never New Year's Eve.

one. The meaning of this word when used emphatically is best illustrated by examples: as, *The room was in one* (or, *one state of) confusion,* i.e. There was horrible confusion; or, *as soon as he said he couldn't go, there was one argument,* i.e. There was a terrific argument. One-**one,** one at a time, as, *one-one blows kill old cow;* and one **time,** rightaway, as, *I going post the letter one time,* are colloquialisms. Also to be noted are (i) the use of one meaning *by oneself,* as, *He can do the job* **his** one; and, (ii) meaning *own* as *This is he one, that is you one.* In (ii) the word is pronounced "wun"; in all other instances, "wawn". Sometimes with the meaning of commonplace, of no account, as, *She treat she husband like if he was one little boy.*

one-side. Aside. *Put it one-side for me.* Also used instead of one-sided, crooked, as *Her hat stand one-side.*

onliest for only is common.

opetin. (Verb.) Open. A curious example of metathesis in which the words "open it" have become transposed. *I can't opetin it.*

opinated. A corruption of "opinionated", and much more frequently used than the correct word.

ordinary. "Common, vulgar, unrefined – 1791", S.O.E.D., is no longer modern Standard English, but it is in this sense that the word is most frequently used, as, *He behaves so ordinary you wouldn't think he comes from a respectable home.*

organ dust. A sort of humorously affectionate soubriquet for coo-coo which is made from corn meal. The grains of the meal greatly resemble the seed-like debris which betrays the presence of the wood-ant or wood-worm in furniture. Why the organ, of all sorts of woodwork, should have been chosen to exemplify the comparison, is obscure. Perhaps it goes to show that two of the chief delights of the Barbadian are a love of his stomach and of church music.

out. Artists are sometimes requested to *draw out a person,* i.e. to sketch him; and a completed exercise book is said to be *written out. Out it off,* rub it off, erase it.

outlorded. (Outlawed?) Rude, intractable, good-for-nothing.

outman. *A man in the canes,* an outlaw, a bogey man.

out-out. To put out, extinguish. See **COMPOUND REDUNDANT.**

outside. Illegitimate, as, *outside child.*

outside ticket. *I got a outside ticket to the show to-night* would be a facetious way of saying that the speaker intended watching the show from outside, through a window perhaps.

over. (Noun). In the plural, things left over, as, *When you finish the job, please for the overs.* (Verb). *When the show overring?*

overhead. (Cricket). A fieldsman placed almost directly behind the bowler, serving as both deep long off and deep long on. Such a fieldsman is also said to be **in the country.**

overhead shower. A sharp shower of comparatively brief duration.

overlook. To mark errors in proof-sheet or examination papers, to look over.

own-way. (Adjective). Headstrong, or stubborn: *An own-way child.*

P.

pack-all. A sort of suit-case made of two deep trays of basketwork, one of which fits easily into the other, and into which clothes etc. are packed.

paddyman. (obsolete). One of the rank and file of the old B.W.I. Regiment.

paipsey. (School slang.) Of insipid or unattractive appearance.

palang-palang. A shout vented by cricket enthusiasts when barracking a fast bowler. The reason for this chant of disapproval is that the fast bowler in question being regarded as completely innocuous and depending solely on speed, needs only a bell to be attached to his arm so that the batsman being thus warned of his approach can afford to play his deliveries without caring where the ball is pitched. The 'palang-palang' represents the sound of the bell.

palisade, palisadin'. An ornamental wooden fence in front of a cottage.

pamper, pampah. I have never quite discovered the exact meaning of this word which occurs in expressions like *If I catch you I'll make you pamper,* or, *The batsmen made the bowlers pamper.*

Panama man. (Obsolete). A term applied during the early years of the present century to a labourer who returned from Panama where the canal was being constructed, and, who, either by dress or opulence, attracted attention. Hence, also Panama **money.**

pancart. A wheelbarrow.

pan-sugar. "The sugar formed on implements and vessels (particularly the oscillator) in an old-fashioned open-process sugar factory." *The Harrisonian, July, 1925.* Such sugar-factories have now disappeared, and pan-sugar is a thing of the past.

pappy. (i) Although mammy (mother) is listed in the C.O.D., it is surprising that its masculine counterpart is not. (ii) "Of the nature or consistence of pap" S.O.E.D. Not in the C.O.D.

parade. Used metaphorically to denote doing as one likes, or having matters all one's way; as, *The batsmen paraded on the bowling;* or, making a great display of anger, as, *If the old man finds out, he is going to parade.*

parrot-toed. (pronounced "paratoed".) With the toes turned inward when walking.

part. In conjunction with *which:* where. As *Which part get hurt?*

partly. Almost, nearly. *He partly killed the thief.*

parts. Any Friday in Bridgetown one may overhear planters referring to the number of parts they have had during the week, references usually made in despondent tones. For instead of inches of rain, they quote only the decimal parts of an inch that have fallen.

passage. Occasionally used to mean shed-roof.

pass out. To pass a car moving in the same direction. *As soon as we get on the straight road I going try to pass him out.* Jokes are not given or even cracked: they are passed. *We sat around on the verandah passing jokes.*

passover. An apoplectic stroke, usually of a comparatively mild nature.

paste out. Most probably a metaphor taken from kite-making, may mean either (i) dressed up to the nines, as, *I saw Maude in the Park, and she was paste out pretty;* or, (ii) give a good dressing down to someone, as, *The boss paste him out.*

pea-eye. Peep at. *I see he pea-eyeing me.*

peck. A pick, or pick-axe.

peeny, pinny. Tiny. Also **peeny-weeny.**

pee-whittler. ("Elainea pagana barbadensis. Cory.) ... a bird at first glance resembling a sparrow, but of a redder brown, with a longer tail and lighter underparts ... its loud piercing note – *peewit peewit, peewit* – often betrays its presence. It is a member of the family of New World Flycatchers ... and the Barbadian bird is only a sub-species of a species found from Grenada to the Virgin Islands." *Mrs. F.C.K. Anderson: Some Observations on the Birds of Barbados. B.M.H.S.*

peggers. (Nursery.) Teeth.

pelt. Properly "to assail with missiles", is often used instead of the more common *shy,* as, *He pelted a stone at me.*

pension. A copper coin. *Please, mister, please for a pension!* was a frequent demand made on motorists by small boys in country districts. Due to either the low purchasing power of the copper coin, or lack of co-operation on the part of motorists, the demand is no longer heard.

people. Often used as an indefinite pronoun, as, *Why you don't come out of the people shop?* or even *Why you don't leave people 'lone nuh?* when someone has interfered with the speaker. Also to be noted is the phrase *You is people too?,* i.e., Do you consider yourself someone of consequence?

peradventure. This word, now archaic in Standard English, is still in use locally.

perjohnny. A "poor white".

perlix. (Verb.) To show off, to display one's technical skill ostentatiously. Possibly a corruption of *prolix,* the meaning of lengthiness and tediousness being confused with that of accomplishment.

person. Used instead of *one* in compounds like *no-person,* and *some-person.*

petties. A crab's claws.

physsie. (Slang). Applied to physical culturists, weight lifters, and so forth, as, *Boy, don't interfere with him: he is a physsie.*

pick is still in use with its old meaning of pilfer: a housewife will tell you that her servant picks. On one occasion a man accused of stealing potatoes indignantly repudiated the charge: *I was not stealing, your worship. I was only picking.* But it would be unfair, I suppose, to impute dishonesty to anyone who told you he was *getting a little pick at Mr. X's store:* he would mean that he had got a small job here. (School slang). Crib. The use of the expression "to pick one's teeth" may be best gathered from the following example: *She tell me all kinds o'things, but child, I in't even pick my teeth:* that is: "I didn't even open my mouth – not even wide enough to pick my teeth," pick a **lime**: see **lime**; pick **wilks**: pick whelks, little molluses found on rocks by the sea-shore, the phrase being used facetiously as the last resort of the unemployed, as, *He must be picking wilks now since he lost his job.*

picnicking. A term used when boats, having found a good fishing bank, all collect there and make an unusually good catch.

pick-ups. Child's game played with pebbles; known in the U.S., I believe, as "jacks".

picky-head. Applied to Negress who wears her hair short.

piece. (i) In compounds only, a field; as, **cane**-piece, **grass**-piece; etc. (ii) "Technical term used by laundresses who charge a specified amount for washing a certain number of garments. A piece: a shirt, or small table-cloth. A white suit: 4 pieces, a large table-cloth, 1½ pieces, etc." *The Harrisonian July 1925.*

pier-head. Not listed in the C.O.D., but defined in the S.O.E.D., as "The outward or seaward end of a pier 1682." The word is used only with reference to the pier situated at the entrance to the Careenage in Bridgetown.

pig-breakfast. Midday meal in which the principal dish is roast sucking pig.

piggin. Perhaps the definition as given in the S.O.E.D. might best describe this outmoded article: "Chiefly *dial*, 1554. A small pail, esp. a wooden one with one stave longer than the rest serving as a handle..." A word seldom heard to-day.

pilot. (Slang.) Pimp, procurer.

pimploe. Not listed in either the C.O.D. or the S.O.E.D. Originally applied to the thorny agave, or Spanish Needle; cf.

> See the bright verdure of those evergreens,
> The rustling bamboo, and the pimploe screens...
> Chapman: *Barbados and other Poems.*

But the word has now come to mean a thorn, or prickle, and is usually pronounced **plimploe,** or **plimpler.**

ping-pong. A small photograph, such as is used for passport requirements.

pipe. Tap. *He got the house fix up nice enough: a pipe in every single bedroom.*

piss-to-windward. I hope I may be excused including this rather indelicate compound, but it is so expressive of lubberly ineptitude that it would be a pity to ignore it, *Good God, George, look what this p.-to-w. done with your new saw!*

pistol ball. This relic of duelling days is now reserved, metaphorically for missives only. *He told me he'd sent the man a pistol ball of a letter.*

pisstoratically. (Slang.) Needing no definition, and applied to a certain stage of drunkenness.

pivvy. Used to denote the tiniest degree of measurement; as, *Move the nail a pivvy to the right.*

plant. *If I plant you, you will grow?* This inexplicable metaphor which was brought to my attention recently is in common use, and, usually addressed to children, simply means "Will you do me a little favour"?

planter's punch. "Into a half-pint tumbler put 1 gill of rum, 2 dashes of Angostura bitters, 1½ teaspoonfuls of sugar, a little fresh green lime or a slice of lemon. Add cracked ice, and fill up the glass with water, grate a little nutmeg on top". *A Souvenir of Barbados.*

plate. Sometimes applied to a gramophone record.

play-play. Make believe. *It was only a play-play wolf in the film.*

please. It would be difficult to give a comprehensive list of the many idiomatic uses of the word. *No please* would strike oddly on English ears, and such expressions as *Please for salt,* or *Please for a pass* may give some idea of its uses. Nor should the expression *Please God* (i.e. if it pleases God) be overlooked. *I'll see you tomorrow, please God.*

pleg. A corruption of plague, and applied to boils and sores; as *I have a pleg on my ankle.*

plimpler, plimploe. See **pimploe.**

pocket pistol. (Slang). Roasted corn on the cob.

points. See **mill**-points.

poison lizard. Applied to the **wood-slave** or gecko, or **white lizard**, which is quite harmless though somewhat repulsive -looking.

polion. A tarpaulin.

Pollard' cellar. To say that someone is *sleeping in Pollard' cellar* implies that the person referred to has no settled place of abode, but that, like the turkey (to use another common saying), he sleeps *wherever night catch him.* This reference may be to the large 'hurricane-shelter cellar' at Pollard's Plantation in the parish of St. Philip.

pompasset. (Accented on the last syllable.) An expressive word denoting ostentatiousness in dress. Frequently used in conjunction with perlix; as, *The boys were perlixing and pompassetting at the fair in the park.*

pond-fly. Dragon fly, the larva of which is known as a **pond-dog.**

pond-boat. A toy boat.

pooch. (Slang.) An old motor car.

pooma. (Slang.) An old motor car.

poor-great. Applied to persons who have come down in the world, but who still try to maintain their former dignity. The word is used in a derogatory sense, and implies an element of snobbishness as well.

poor man's pork. Broad-leaf thyme.

poor-rakey. An expressive adjective denoting scrawniness.

pop. To break suddenly, not necessarily with any noise; as, *Pop the thread*, or, *The needle gone and pop.*

poppet, poppit. A laughing-stock. *She look a regular poppit in that dress, though, nuh?* Never used as a term of endearment.

pot, Black-pot, soot; pot-**fish,** fish caught in a **fish-pot;** to **go** to pot, to run to seed, to fail; as, *All his great plans gone to pot.* **Pepper** pot; the following recipe is taken from *West Indian Cookery: E. Phyllis Clarke:*– "Clean and cut meat (1 oxtail or tough fowl duck or any game in season; 3 lb. fresh lean pork; 1 lb. pickled pork) into small pieces. Put in large conaree (casserole) and cover with plenty of water. Cover and simmer for 2 hr. Add peppers (tied in a net bag), thyme, sliced onions, sugar and casseripe (cassareep). Simmer again till meat is tender. Boil up every day to prevent food turning bad. Add fresh meat from time to time (the meat must be seasoned and nothing starchy may be put in, or pepper pot will turn sour)." An interesting note from *A Souvenir of Barbados: Gladys Skinner*: "Cassareep is made in British Guiana from the juice of the cassava. British Guiana is the real home of the pepper pot. In the old days every plantation had one with a locked cover (a necessary precaution it was). 'Friends have arrived unexpectedly – Please lend us your pepper pot', was an ordinary appeal from one plantation to another. Legend has it that the same pepper pot would be kept going for years!"

potato. Always the sweet potato, which is not to be confused with the **English** or **Irish** potato. There are many varieties of the sweet potato, and the local names, fast dying out, might form the subject of a monograph; e.g., Caroline Lee, White Gilks, Kickup Jinnies, Six Weeks, Pumpkin Stewards, Red Cannon Balls, Black Rock, Stafford, Play Hell Galore, etc. etc.

pouch. A tube. *I brought a pouch of toothpaste.*

poxy. Pocky.

presently. Although not used colloquially in its archaic sense, i.e., "at present", yet a frequent standby of journalists as, *Mr. X. presently on sick leave, will be resuming duties ... etc.*

press. Properly, a large usually shelved cupboard (C.O.D.), but frequently used to mean a wardrobe.

pretensive. Of Badian origin, and not to be confused with "pretentious", implies an artificial putting on of airs and graces, a studied insincerity.

pretty. Is usually pronounced to rhyme with 'Betty'. As an adverb of degree: thoroughly, as, *Joe beat him up pretty.*

pretty-betty. A speckled peascod. Also applied to a freckled **redleg**.

proddle. To stir the mould in the garden-bed. Hence the **proddler** is the instrument by means of which the job is accomplished, usually one of the prongs of a large garden fork.

PRONUNCIATION. As stated in the Introduction to these notes, pronunciation is outside their scope; but I think that some reference must be made to that peculiarity of local intonation – the accentuation of the former syllable of disyllabic words, and of the former of two monosyllabic words, especially a noun and its epithet. Indeed, in some instances, a word, pronounced in the Barbadian manner, carries quite a different meaning from the word pronounced according to Standard English requirement. Take the word, Scotland, for example. With the accent placed normally the former syllable, it means the country north of England. But by over emphasising this accent, holding on to it, as it were, making the slightest of pauses thereafter, and then allowing the voice to rise ever so slightly for the second syllable, quite a different intonation is achieved, and, too, a word with quite a different meaning: **Scot**-land; the hilly district to the north of Barbados! A few other frequently used words with this varying accentuation which illustrate this difference are: brother and **bro**-ther (a member of some religious sect); sister and **sis**-ter (in the same sense); worker and **wor**-ker (a milliner); copy (verb) and **cop**-y (noun); body and **bod**-y, (person); tailor and **Tay**-lor (proper name). It must be remembered that the Standard English pronunciation of Scotland, brother, sister, worker, and tailor are exceptional; almost every dissyllabic word is pronounced as I have attempted to indicate above. Thus, "There's a golf course at Rockley" would be rendered "there's a **golf**-course at **Rock**-ley," and "Peter, you got cold feet?" **Pe**-ter, you got **cold**-feet?" This over-accentuation together with the subsequent pause, not unnaturally results in the fact that Barbadians speak rather more slowly than other English-speaking communities. It may also be noted in connection with the Barbadian drawl that most vowels sounds tend to be drawn out, and that some of them like O, for example, actually become compound vowel sounds; **O-AH;** as, *boaht* and *goaht* for goat and boat. (See **VOWEL SOUNDS.**) Two other idiosyncrasies of pronunciation may be touched on here, (i) the fact that most Barbadians, even the well-educated, who would not dream of saying "dis" and "dat" for "this" and "that", nevertheless prefer "de" to "the"; and (ii) the tendency to drop off the final consonants of words, like "san" for sand, "hopin" for hoping, "poun" for pound, etc., etc.

prop. The expressive term *propping sorrow* is used with reference to the attitude of someone who is sitting, staring into vacancy, with his chin cupped in his hands, and his elbows propped on his knees, or on the surface of a table, etc. *Child what you propping sorrow for? What trouble you?* Also used as an echo word to express the sound made by the canes as they burst during the intense heat of a cane-fire. *Boy, you can hear the canes propping from here.*

public, The. (Noun). Usually, the Government. *Hey, that tap belong to the public, hear?* or, *When I get old, I don't want to be an expense to the public.*

pull. Cards are never *drawn* from a pack; they are always pulled.

pull-down. (Adjective.) Best explained by an example: *There was a real pull-down row in the rumshop last night.*

pump. (Slang). To get a free ride or drive, as, *I wonder if I can pump a lift to town.*

pumps. Soft shoes, sneakers.

punish. Used intransitively, to suffer. *But look at me here punishing for a drink.*

punk. (Schoolboy slang). A booby, a duffer.

punksey. Spunky.

puppy-eye. A small shell, any one of the species of the genus *Nerita,* used in the making of brooches, ornaments. etc.

puppy skull. Now, I fear, obsolete. A bowler hat.

push breadcart. A euphemism to denote pregnancy. *Hey, I see Doreena like she pushing breadcart.*

pushunder. A euphemism for a chamber-pot, very often pushed under the bed. I have also heard this article referred to as a **guzunda,** a word which I thought at first to refer to some lethal weapon; but its derivation is pretty much the same: it goes *under* the bed.

put. The following idioms may be noted: (i) *The house was very nicely put* **away:** the house was very tastefully furnished; (ii) *I told him I'd go, but I didn't put a* **foot.** I didn't budge; (iii) *The newspaper put it* **on** (or, put it **all over**) *the scheme this morning:*

The newspaper treated the scheme very severely this morning; (iv) *Don't go and put your* **mouth** *on the concert*: Don't bring bad luck on the concert by wishing it ill, or by suggesting that ill may befall it; (v) *She can't help what she doing: somebody put she so:* She has been bewitched by obeah.

Q.

quail. "To fade, wither. Obs. exc. dialect, 1440" S.O.E.D. A quailed plantain leaf (see **conkie**) would be one that had had its moisture dried by holding it over the fire. A wrinkled face is sometimes referred to as being *quailed up.*

quaka-hadja. A small puppet of wood or cardboard with jointed limbs moved with strings, or a person whose movements are jerky and/or awkward. Mr. E. M. Shilstone writes: "John Camden Hotten in *The Slang Dictionary Etymological Historical, and Anecdotal* (Chatto & Windus, London, 174, p.265) defined *quockerwodger* as 'a wooden toy figure which, when pulled by a string, jerks its limbs about. The term is used in a slang sense to signify a pseudo-politician, one whose strings of actions are pulled by somebody else'. Eric Patridge, in his *Dictionary of Slang and Unconventional English* (Macmillan, New York, 1950, p.680) defines Quockerwodger as 'a politician acting upon an outsider's orders' and traces its political connotation to 1859 when it was derived from quocker-wodger, a puppet of strings... My attention has been drawn to the above source of information by Dr. D. C. Mearns, Chief of Manuscripts Division, Library of Congress, Washington, D.C."

quart. Since the introduction of decimal coinage, the 25 cent piece (American quarter) has been termed a quart.

quidney. A preserve made from the seeds of the guava.

R.

rab. (noun.) Used instead of **rabble**, applied contemptuously to the mob. (Adjective) The term **rab land,** used in legal documents, etc, refers to land, usually stony, unfit for agricultural purposes.

race. Frequently used to mean *chase,* as, *Race that stray dog out of the yard!* or, *Race away that dog.*

raft. Occasionally used as a collective noun to denote a crowd, as, *a raft of people.* The S.O.E.D. states "(Chiefly U.S.A.) large floating mass or accumulation of fallen trees, logs, vegetation, ice, etc. Also a dense flock of swimming birds".

rain-bird. (Also Doctor Morris Bird.) "This large bird is often to be seen sitting on telephone wires or dead twigs, from which it flies out at intervals after insects or lizards. It is grey above, with darker head, wings, and tail, and pearly white below, and has a long powerful bill. It is said to have been introduced into the island by Dr. Morris..." *Some Observations on the Birds of Barbados: Mrs. F.C. K. Anderson.*

ram. Ram-**sheep** is preferred to ram (see **COMPOUND REDUNDANT**). A male goat is always called a ram-**goat**.

rat. If you ask a small boy to show you his rat, he will pinch his biceps, provoking a spasm of a muscle; the muscle-spasm is the rat. (Slang.) A prostitute.

rata. The molasses that dripped from the hogshead on to the open floor of the sugar **stanchion**. This molasses acted as a trap for all sorts of vermin, especially rats, hence the name. Black Strap molasses is still known as rata, but it is now prepared under more hygienic conditions.

rather. (Verb.) Prefer; as, *I rather this one,* or, *He rathered stay at home.*

ray-mouth. Really *rear-mouth.* A condition due to malnutrition when the mouth has the appearance of rare, or imperfectly cooked meat.

razzy. (Slang.) Shabby, down-at-heel.

reading-book. A story book as distinct from copybook, exercise book, picture book, lesson book, etc.

reckon. Change is not counted; it is reckoned.

red. Frequently used to refer to a mulatto or "near-white", and implying a certain degree of contempt, as, *You know the good-for-nothing red man that lives round the corner?*

red-leg. A poor-white. The following extract from evidence given before the Royal Commission in 1897 gives this definition: "they are largely the failures of families who have now been in some cases over three centuries in the island, and so far from getting black, they get bloodless in appearance, and the sun has given those parts of the body exposed to it a colour which finds its expression in the local name of red-legs."

regulars. The small, harmless black ants which are to be found in almost every house.

rein back. To bend the upper part of the body backwards as though under the influence of reins. E.g. *When the ball got up suddenly, the batsman reined back and cut it for four.*

reneg(u)e. Now archaic English, but still used locally in its original sense of repudiate or deny.

repetition. It is a common tendency to repeat the adjective by way to emphasis, a double repetition being equivalent to a comparative, and a triple, to a superlative; as, *He was an old old man,* and, *He was an old old old man.* The same device is employed with the adverb: *He ran down the road fast, fast,* and *He ran down the road fast, fast, fast.*

rest off. The Barbadian rests, or rather rests himself, at night, but by day he rests off from his work.

reverend. (Noun). A parson. *There was three reverends at the wedding.*

reverse back. Cars are reversed *back;* animals, backed back.

rice. (verb). Support, feed, maintain, as, *Think I taking any orders from you? You does rice me?* The speaker, of course, is a woman.

rid. For some reason or other, one does not get rid of anything: one gets **the** rid of it.

rider. (i) Person who gets a free ride on a lorry. On many lorries the sign *No riders allowed* is much in evidence. (ii) A tooth which pushes its way over another through the side of the gum.

riffle. A meeting of two currents, a tidal race. As this confluence is attended with much churning of foam, the word has also come to refer to a large school of fish lashing about in the water. The S.O.E.D. states "A rapid. U.S. 1796".

ring a bell. To cry out loud; as, *He ran down the road ringing a bell.*

ring-jointed. Double-jointed.

ripping-iron. (Slang). A jacket with a slit up the back.

roach. Cockroach. M. J. Chapman in his **Barbados and other Poems** writes: "The obsene roaches gathered from their holes".

rockinengine. A steam roller.

rock-stone. A stone of any size.

rookety. A pleasant and expressive combination of "rocky" and "rickety", usually employed with reference to roads and tracks.

roost. The proverbial expression, "rule the roast", is always rendered in Barbadian as *rule the roost*, which latter image is certainly more apt. Such an alteration reminds me of a schoolboy's version of *"one swallow doesn't make a summer"*: one swallow doesn't make a supper. But this rendering of the well-known proverb, though more applicable to local conditions, has never become common currency.

rose tree trimmer. This charmingly ironic euphemism is applied to one who pursues the unsavoury profession of cleaning latrines.

round shilling. A term no longer in vogue, which was used with reference to the silver coin of that denomination. Most probably due to the fact that, until the introduction of the English coin in the middle of the nineteenth century, the old "currency shilling" was, like the dollar before 1938, "a unit of account without a corresponding unit of exchange". Dr. Ida Greaves' *Money and Currency in Barbados, Journal of the B.H.M.S., Vol. XIX No. 4 Vol. XX Nos. 1 & 2* is well worth consulting. See also **fisherman's penny,** and **tuppence.**

row. (Verb). *He rowed them all off in front of him.* He arranged them in rows.

rumfle. A portmanteau word formed from rumple and ruffle, and used much more frequently than either of its components.

rummie. A drunkard.

rumshop. Usually a small shop where rum and some other alcoholic drinks are sold, together with such commodities as bread, cheese, sliced ham, etc., and a place where men gather to discuss the topics of the day. The rumshop, which might be classified as a modest "pub", is to be found not only in Barbados, but throughout the Caribbean. It is strange that the word is not listed in the C.O.D., Webster's, or any of the standard dictionaries.

runt. It is interesting to note that the sense in which this word is chiefly used, "a small pig, especially the smallest in a litter", is classified by the S.O.E.D. as "dialect and U.S. 1841".

rush. (Slang). To have a crush on a girl, as, *Who's the girl your brother's rushing now?*

S.

saddlepatch,-piece. A saddle-shaped patch on the seat of the trousers. Many pairs of trousers have had their use considerably lengthened by the addition of this patch; indeed, sometimes the saddle-patch is sewn on before the trousers are worn. The way in which such a patch is regarded is shewn in the old bit of doggerel:

> A patch on the crotch
> Is nothing much;
> A patch on the knee
> Shows povertee.

said. Frequently used in conversation in the sense of same, named or mentioned before, as, *He is the said man I saw yesterday,* or, *That is the said thing I was saying.*

sails. See **mill-sails.**

saki-winkie. A saki is "any of several South American monkeys of the genus Pitheca, having a bushy non-prehensile tail and long hair which usually forms a beard on the chin and ruff around the face", *Webster's International Dictionary.* The component *winkie* seems to be a local addition.

sal. (Slang.) Pal.

salad. Lettuce is nearly always called salad.

salivate. Properly, affected by sialogogue, such as mercury, which produces excess flow of salivation; locally, the ill-effects produced by eating acid fruit while in this condition, and applied especially to persons suffering from defective pigmentation, popularly supposed to be the result of salivation.

salt. The most popular of the many slang terms used to refer to intoxicated persons. Cf. pickled. Salted?

salt-fish. Always salted cod, an article of the staple diet of every true Ba'dian.

Sam Cow and the Duppy. Tom, Dick, and Harry.

sandbox. The sandbox tree, Nura Crepitans Euphorbiaceae. "...the woody fruit covering, with seeds extracted, was formerly used as a sand sprinkler in lieu of blotting paper." *Garden Book of Barbados.* Filled with lead, the sandbox "fruit" is used as a paperweight.
    There is a little explosion when the ripe fruit on the tree bursts open scattering the segments containing the seeds; and when this happens there is an old saying still in vogue that a lizard-wedding has just taken place.

sand-side. The beach. *She has gone down to the sand-side for fish.* Sand-side **lawyer:** one pretending to have a knowledge of law.

sangaree. "The word sangaree is of Spanish origin denoting the blood colour of the drink, which was made of Madina wine, lime juice, sugar, and spice." Note attached to a sangaree **bowl** at the Barbados Museum.

santapee. The phonetic rendering in Ba'dian of centipede.

sankey-malankey. See **sawney-malawney.**

sawney-malawney. A lackadaisical person. The adjective, sawney, is listed in the S.O.E.D. as "1805. Foolish; foolishly sentimental:"

science. "Now especially (somewhat jocularly) with reference to pugilism. 1785"(S.O.E.D.), was used locally with particular application to the art of **stick-licking,** or fencing with sticks, once a very popular sport. The story is told of the first winner of the Barbados Scholarship in science being approached by a resident of one of the remote parishes, who requested him to give him some lessons in the manly art.

scissor-tail, swizzle-tail. (Slang). The old-fashioned cut-away coat.

scoopinickie. (Obsolete). A playful term used in addressing small boys up to twenty years ago, as, *Run along there you little scoopinickie.* In 1821 Marcus Escopiniche, who styled himself The Marquis EscoPiniche, and who was possibly something of a "character", was licensed in Barbados as professor and teacher of languages. Why the corruption of his name should have lingered on in its application to small boys is not known.

scotch. "1601... *trans.* To block or wedge (a wheel, log, gate, etc.) so as to keep from moving or slipping." Used intransitively locally it denotes to obtain a foothold by digging one's heels into the ground or otherwise obtaining a *scotch.* (Noun).

Scotland. Pronounced in the Ba'dian manner (see **PRONUNCIA-TION**), the name given to the hilly district in the north-eastern part of the island. Scotland **johnny**, a red-leg.

scrambler. A cane-hoist on a sugar factory.

scratches. Two little horizontal parallel strokes, like the symbol *equal to*, used by schoolchildren to signify that nothing remains after subtracting.

screel. Applicable to the high-pitched screeching of children, as *The children were yelling and screeling*. George Lamming, in *The Castle of my Skin*, uses the word to describe the piercing sound of a whistle; "At the same hour every morning the whistle screel shot up like an alarm through the rumbling of cart wheels".

screeler. Fishermen looking for dolphin carry out a small wooden raft which they throw overboard and let drift in a likely area so that the fish may gather round.

scrid. A small portion; usually occurring in phrases as, *There wasn't a scrid* (of cloth, etc.) *left over*.

scrip. A short informal letter, usually folded over and not enclosed in an envelope. "Obs. except dialect. 1608. I. A small piece or scrap (of paper, etc.) 2. Scrip (of a pen); A small scrap of writing 1710", states the S.O.E.D.

scrubbers. A name given to small bands of strolling musicians at Christmas-time. Their instruments were of the most rudimentary type, and their leader would, after they had played a couple of hymn-tunes, appeal to the householder for some reward. These speeches, as they were called, were usually delivered in rhyme, the following being a good example.

> As I was passing through Joe's River
> My tender heart began to shiver
> So if you are a cheerful giver,
> Please give me something to warm my liver.

Mr. Louis Lynch's article in *The Barbados Advocate*, (23rd. Dec. 1956) *The Decline of Scrubbing*, to which I am indebted for this information, deals with the subject in detail. The origin of the term is unknown.

scuttler. The greenish brown crab, *Grapsus grapsus*, that abounds on the rocks along the shore.

sea. Occurs in the following combinations, none of which is listed in the C.O.D.; sea-**beef**, the flesh of the whale; sea-**cat**, "A kind of cuttle-fish or octopus caught by probing crevices in the rocks with an iron hook. The unfortunate sea-cat is then turned inside out by the fisherman, and after several days of boiling attains the tenderness and succulence of a piece of leather," *Harrisonian;* sea-**cockroach**, small whitish crustacean that burrows in sandy wave-washed shore-fringe; sea **coconut**, "palm nut brought by the Atlantic current from the northern coast of South America and thrown up on the eastern shore of the island" (Roach; B.M.H.S.); sea-**egg**, the sea urchin. The two commonest varieties are **black** sea egg, or **cobbler**, and the **white** sea egg, which provides Barbadians with one of their most delectable dishes, and which, according to popular lore, is the cause of the islanders' virility and fertility; sea **man-o'war**, the Portuguese man-o'-war; sea-**plate**, mellita sexiesperforata, or keyhole urchin; sea-**spider**, Ophiocoma echinata, fivelegged creature to be found under almost every stone of the coral reef; sea **spry**, seaspray; sea **star**, the large star fish, Oreaster reticularus.

seasoning. (Noun.) Eschalot and other herbs used for seasoning.

second. (Slang.) Close friend.

second-day. Very often when a wedding has taken place on a week-day, the reception is postponed until the following Sunday which is known as the "second day".

see through. Name given to white rum because of its transparency.

self. Often used instead of the emphatic pronoun, as, *the boy self, the thing self, etc.*

semi-demis. In the early years of this century it was the common custom for boys, especially country boys, to wear, before they had been promoted to the distinction of long trousers, semi-demis, i.e. trousers that reached to about the middle of the calf.

serious. "Remarkable, worthy of notice". *Harrisonian. That's a serious score those batsmen made, boy.*

serpent. "A kind of firework which burns with a serpentine motion or flame 1634" (S.O.E.D.), is still much in vogue.

set. Frequently used to mean many, or a lot, as, *There were a set of people standing at the corner. He had a set of money once.* Set **up,** used with reference to the massing of clouds betokening rain, as, *The rain is setting up*; hence, to frown or scowl, as, *He set up his face at me.*

sex. Owing to confusion with the word, sect, it is frequently used in the sense of party, or associate, as, *I ain't no sex with you.*

shades. Sun-glasses.

shag. No doubt from their resemblance to the coarse leaf on the tobacco plant, the dried leaves of banana or plantain are known as shag.

shahyego. An attempted phonetic rendering of sherigo, a small sea crab which is found in shallow water near the beaches and which sometimes nips the toes of bathers. The phrase "snake in the grass" is sometimes translated into Ba'dian as a *shahyego in the* **moss** (sea weed).

shake(a) hand. *I shook my hand at him.* I waved to him.

shakers. Name given to a religious sect whose form of worship involves a series of rhythmic gyrations to the beat of the tambourine.

shak-shak. (See **woman's tongue**). "Albizza Lebbek. Leguminosae. Bare of leaves in the dry season, but covered with long pods which rattle." *Garden Book of Barbados.*

shed-roof. A lean-to, a pent-house.

sheer. Although used correctly in its sense of "pure, undiluted," the phrase *sheer milk* would no doubt strike oddly on English ears.

shell. (Slang). To drive or run fast, as, *He went down the road shelling.* Most likely derived from Shell Motor Spirit.

sherigo. Species of crab (Callinectes diacanthus) found in shallow water off the coast.

she-she. Effeminate, as, *You mean that she-she young man?*

shew. (pronounced shoo). Mistaken for the past tense of show, and frequently used in this sense, as *The caretaker shew us around.* Shew is variant of show, and has shewed as its past tense.

shoe. A bit of canvas or old tyre inserted for support within a badly damaged tyre.

shoot. The expletive *O shoot* is generally indicative of astonishment. (Verb.) In Barbados one does not go surf-riding; one *shoots* **waves.** Or is it 'chutes'?

shun. Now used in Standard English to mean "avoid, keep clear of, aschew", C.O.D., is still employed in its more everyday sense of "evade (a blow, missile) 1667", S.O.E.D., as *He tried to shun the car, and rode into the gutter,* or, *He (cyclist) shunned me just in time.* Noteworthy is the expressive adjective and adverb **shunnafoot,** applied to persons who walk with their toes pointing outwards and their feet, as it were, avoiding each other. *A shunnafoot man, He walks shunnafoot.* Hence **shunna,** used as adverb only.

sick. Still used in its Elizabethan sense of ill or unwell. A sick: a person who is ill. See also **bad** sick, and **new** sick.

side. District, region. He comes from up my side. He was standing side o'me. The word beside, is rarely, if ever used. See **wh'side.**

silk cotton. Not listed in the C.O.D. The S.O.E.D. states "1. The silky elastic down or fibre obtained from various bombinaceous and other tropical trees. 2. Silkcotton **tree,** any of the various species of tropical trees belonging to the genera Bombax, Eriodendron, Ochroma, and Pachira, which produce silk cotton. 1712."

silk grass. "Applied to various species of aloe, agave, or yucca, or the fibre derived from these 1753," S.O.E.D. Not listed in the C.O.D.

silvers. Articles made of silver, especially forks, spoons, etc. *I hasn't cleaned the silvers yet, ma'am.*

singing. (Noun). This singing is nowadays quite a popular form of entertainment. Singings usually take place on Sunday afternoons when the members of some friendly society or club, after a prelude of hymn singing, resort to dancing to the accompaniment of a steel band.

singing angel. A kite which, "provided with an octagon of 'bulls' around its perimeter", produces when aloft a melodious humming. Mr. Louis Lynch's *The Barbados Book* should be consulted by those interested in the various types of kites that were once the pride and joy of Barbadian youth at Eastertide.

single up. A few days ago a friend and I were walking abreast along a pavement in Bridgetown when we were addressed by a rather excited pedestrian immediately behind us to *single up*. I do not know if this expression is in common use, but is certainly very expressive.

sitting. A seat. At funerals and weddings people sometimes pool together in order to hire a car. The seat thus booked is called a sitting.

sitting breeches. Callers who have outstayed their welcome are said to be wearing sitting breeches.

sittoo. (Noun). Properly, set to: a **stick-licking** tournament (Rare).

size. With the adverb, up, to move up: *Young man, size up and give the lady a seat.*

skin. (Noun). The terms **clear**-skin (fair), and **smooth**-skin (sleek), are in common use. *Who's that nice piece o' skin?* is sometimes used with reference to the attractive young female. (Verb). To skin **cuffins** or **cuffums,** to turn somersaults; to skin **out,** to turn inside out, as, *He skinned out his pocket;* to skin **up** one's face, to make a wry face, as, *Don't skin up your face at good food, child;* to skin one's **teeth,** to grin; hence the noun **skin-teet,** as, in the proverbial expression, *Every skin-teet' ain't a laugh.*

97

skinners. Children learning to write are taught to make *pot-hooks and skinners.* Skimmers?

skinsman. A Casanova.

sliders. Old-fashioned long underpants or drawers.

sling. In the old "open process" of sugar manufacture, the cane juice just before crystallisation, became a thick viscous mass known as sling.

slip-and-dip. A not inappropriate term for a dish of eddoes and shad.

slip-slop. A sandal made of a wooden sole and a leather strap. An echo word derived from the noise made by the wearer when walking.

small bones. *She is making small bones:* She is pregnant.

snowball. A concoction made of "shaved" ice, flavoured usually with a bright red syrup!

so. Sometimes used for so long as; *You can go out so you don't stay long.* The Barbadian expression, for so, conveys quite a different meaning from the Trinidadian. *I went for a walk for so.* I had no particular reason for going for a walk. The word often means that way in that direction. When a visitor asks to be directed to a place, he will be told *You go so, and then so, and swing so...* each 'so' being accompanied by a graphic gesture of the hand indicating whether left or right, as the case may be. But sometimes the gesture is considered unnecessary, so that the visitor is simply directed to "go so".

societ. (Pronounced so-sy-it.) To associate. *Me and him don't societ.*

soft stone, also referred to as **sawed stone,** is the name given to the limestone blocks quarried locally, to distinguish it from hard stone or rubble, which in former days was considered preferable for building. But as the stone is actually sawed into blocks, there is perhaps some cause for the confusion in the names.

soldier crab. Hermit crab.

solid. The phrase 'bar solid' indicates that strong drink will be served.

somebody. In referring to the cost of an article, say three dollars and some cents, the speaker will say *This cost three dollars somebody,* instead of, as might be expected, three dollars something.

sometimish. The sometimish acquaintance is one to be avoided, for sometimes he is all smiles and affability at other times distant, almost supercilious, in his manner: in short, insincere.

sooner. (Noun). A mongrel. On asking on one occasion why a "sooner", I was told,

He'd sooner bark than bite,
And sooner run than fight.

soul, soulie. This might be regarded as the feminine form of **bo** and **bosie,** employed as a nominative of address, and implying sympathy and/or familiarity, as *What happen to you, soul?* Also **soulie gal.** Soul-**case**: the human frame, as, *Look at me worrying out my soul-case.*

sow. (Slang, now obsolete.) A frock coat. In the early years of the present century when frock-coats and top hats were a common sight on Sunday, gentlemen thus attired were often requested by street urchins to "Give her some mash". I have not been able to discover the origin of the term. Sow-pig: see **COMPOUND REDUNDANT.**

spalter. To split or splinter, applied to brittle wood. Cognate with spalt "dialect. 1733. To split, tear, splinter". S.O.E.D.

Spanish needles. Yucca aloifolia. Liliaceae. Noted in the S.O.E.D. as "Spanish dagger".

spar. (Slang). Chum or pal.

sparrow-bird. See **COMPOUND REDUNDANT**:

spawgee. A poor backra, or **redleg**. Probably derived from *The Spa*, a plantation in the Scotland district.

spawn. Span with the outstretched hand. *It is so wide I don't think I can spawn it.*

speculator. Especially applied to one who deals in buying and selling cattle and other live stock.

Speightstown compliment. A left-handed compliment. Was it because in former days Speightstonians were supposed to be less urbane in their manners than dwellers in the metropolis?

speedy corks. A name given in some parishes, I am informed, to the metal caps or stoppers of the popular sweet **drinks.**

spell. To beg for some favour or object by means of broad hints, as, *I can see you're spelling to go to the party, but you're wasting your time.*

spend. *How did you spend your time this afternoon?* does not mean "How did you pass your time this afternoon?", but "How did you enjoy yourself this afternoon?"

spider. A wheeled metal contrivance used for carting puncheons. The puncheon is suspended between the wheels by means of an arched frame. Cf. "Nautical. An iron outrigger to keep blocks clear of the ship's side. Cf. spider-hoop. 1860", S.O.E.D. *Webster's New International* lists "spider cart. A kind of lightly constructed cart." *The B.M.H.S., Vol. XXIII No. 1* states: "The 'Spider' was invented by the late George Herbert when he was employed by DaCosta & Co. in their sugar depot in the early eighties of the last century. It was invented to carry a hogshead of sugar weighing about one ton. Afterwards, smaller vehicles of identical design were used to transport puncheons of molasses or syrup.

spraddle. A very effective portmanteau word formed from sprawl and straddle to denote an undignified position, as *Nowadays people in the bus won't move round and you does have to spraddle over them.* Also the facetious **catspraddle.**

spranksious. Friskly, lively, as, *That's a spranksious horse there.*

spree-boy. Gay young fellow who is disinclined to work.

squizzy, squizzyazzy-voo. A squiggle.

squulch is much preferred to either squelch or squash. *I nearly got squulched in the crowd.*

stake out. It is a familiar sight in Barbados to see animals, especially sheep and goats, staked out to graze, i.e. attached by a rope to an iron stake driven into the ground. So the phrase is used metaphorically, and a fielding eleven given a good sunning may be said to have been staked out.

stanchion. Properly "an upright bar, stay, or support, as for a ship's deck, awning, etc." (S.O.E.D.), but applied locally to a building, sugar-stanchion, provided with floor of transverse beams through the apertures of which the molasses from the hogsheads drips on to the shallow cemented tank below.

stand. The past tense, stood, is frequently confused with the past tense of the verb, stay, as, *I stood in the country for a week.* See **sticky.**

stand pipe. As I mentioned in the Introduction, there are many words which the Barbadian regards as Standard English only to discover later that he has been in error; thus, although I listed 'pipe' as a tap, I omitted this compound, the source of water for those who do not have it piped into their homes. The stand pipe is to be found by the wayside in every village and is the meeting place for exchange of news and gossip.

step out. To leave one's occupation for a short while, as, *Mistress I just stepping out for a minute.* A correspondent writes: "The above request was made to me when new to Barbados by a servant who, being given leave to do so, disappeared for the rest of the day. She was very indignant next morning when I expressed my feelings on the matter. I later learned to impose a time limit on the stepping out. Like **just now**, it would seem to denote an elastic measurement of time."

stew dumplings. Another name for **conkies.**

stick. At parties cakes are not cut, they are stuck. I suppose that to the persons concerned in the procedure the sticking is of more immediate interest than the cutting.

stick-lash. A blow with a stick.

stick-licking. The art of fencing with sticks. See **science.**

sticky. *If your ma find out what you done, you going to stand sticky, boy:* i.e., you'll find yourself in an awkward situation.

stock. Properly a collective noun, live stock, the word is applied to any single animal commonly found on a farm. The plural is stocks. *Mary, you feed the stocks yet to-day?*

stomach-bone. Chest as, *You going catch cold exposing your stomach-bone like that, hear?*

stone-bruise. In former days when the majority of the population went barefoot, bruises, in the correct sense of the term, occasioned by stones were very common.

stop bram. To stop dead.

store. Always, as in the U.S., a large shop.

Storm, The. The hurricane of September 1898. Storm-**carpenter,** a very inexperienced person who attempts a job of carpentry. Most householders would find themselves called upon to do carpenters' jobs after a storm.

strand up. Reduced to strands or shreds, as, *His house was all strand up after the storm.*

stranna. A term given to the whirling, zigzag motion of a kite that has got temporarily out of control. Hence, applied figuratively to one who is bewildered or disconcerted. *The examining lawyer had poor Jones in a stranna to-day.*

strat. Used as both noun and verb; an abbreviated form, I suppose, of stratagem, to denote deception of some kind, as (i) *He tried to put a strat on me.* (ii) *Man, who you think you stratting?*

strings. Sinews, tendons. *This rheumatism got all my strings draw(n).*

study. To give thought to, to pay attention to, as *I didn't study I would have to do this,* or, *I have got to go now and study feeding the fowls.* The noun **studiation** may be noted: *Too much studiation can set a man mad.*

stuff. Rubbish. Hence stuff-**box**, a receptacle for depositing rubbish and refuse, and stuff-**cart**, or cart for collecting same. Stuffed up, suffering from a cold in the head.

stump. Stub. He stumped his toe on the stone.

stupse. See chupse.

suck. A vertical shaft sunk in a depression of a field for the purpose of carrying off surplus water during the rain season; also suck-**well.** **Suck-the-well-dry,** a card game. To suck the **teeth,** to **chupse,** or **stupse.**

sugar-bird. "The sugar-bird is slaty black above and on the throat, and yellow on the breast, belly, and rump: it has a conspicuous white stripe over the eye, a white border to the tail, and coral-red patch at the base of the bill, probably only in the breeding male. The family of the Honey-creepers to which it belongs is found all over the West Indies and in South America." F.C.K. Anderson *Some Observations on the Birds of Barbados. B.M.H.S.*

sugar-cakes. Locally made sweets of coconut and sugar sold by sweet vendors.

Sugar Hill. Name of a country plantation. Many a bowler who has been severely punished by some batsman has had chanted at him *So and so come from Sugar Hill.*

supposed. Frequently used as a periphrasis for the verb to be. Thus the sentence *He is supposed to be a carpenter* would not necessarily throw any doubt on the capability of the workman in question.

surge. Used metaphorically to denote having one's way, as, *Now his pa come back, Joe can't surge.*

swale. Noted in the S.O.E.D. as "A hollow, low place," this word is applied to the wide depression or dip in some country roads that serves as a drain. As the occupants of a car when travelling over one of these depressions tend to bow their heads involuntarily swales are also known as **thank-you-ma'ams.**

swamps. There are not many natural swamps in the island, but many artificial ones have been constructed as a lure to the many migratory birds which visit us during the **hurricane months.** Hence swamp-**bird:** any such migratory bird.

swank. Slang term for a drink of sugar and water.

sweet. Occasionally used as a euphemism for intoxicated. Sweet **drink,** a soft drink; sweet **man** (obsolescent), a dandy; sweet **mouth** and sweet **talk,** flattery, blandishment; hence, **sweeten,** flatter. In this connection, the local proverb, *Wha' sweeten goat-mout' bu'n he tail* may be noted.

sweetheart. (i) A burr. (ii) A sort of sweet bread. (iii) The little whitish blemish formed on the fingernail.

sweetie pills. A familiar term used over a long period of years by countless Barbadian mothers who have bought homeopathic pillules from the beneficent Mr. Yearwood for the ailments of their children.

sweeties. Sweets are bought in a shop, sweeties from the vendor's (sweet-**seller,** or sweetie-**woman**) tray. There are many kinds of sweeties, made chiefly of sugar, coconut, and/or peanuts, and are known severally as sugar cakes, sugar cocks, nut cakes, glass cakes (peanut brittle), sweetie boots (these are flavoured with ginger), sweetie balls, etc.

sweet lime. Triphasia trifolia. Rubiaceae. Unexcelled as a hedge.

sweetskin bucky. This, I am informed, is the equivalent of saga boy in some of the windward parishes.

swing. Motorists always swing, not turn, to the right or left as the case may be. The Englishman might think that such an operation involves some risk, since, properly speaking, swinging would imply a sharp, even violent turn; but when he notes that pedestrians also swing a corner, and this without resort to acrobatics, his fears vanish.

swinge. Singe. "Now dialect and U.S. 1590." S.O.E.D.

swipe. (School slang.) Pinch, pilfer.

swizzle. A word now replaced by cocktail. "A name of various compounded drinks 1813," states the S.O.E.D., which also defines swizzle-**stick** "a stick used for stirring drink into a froth." The swizzle-stick has been replaced by the cocktail-shaker, but the following definition from *The Harrisonian* reminds us of its forgotten glory: "A small nutmeg branch whose shoots radiate from a central stalk. This is cut, trimmed, and peeled, and has an aromatic odour. When made to revolve by rubbing between the palms of the hands, it speedily mixes the ingredients of the cocktail into a foaming nectar." The C.O.D. offers no comment on swizzles and swizzle-sticks.

sword, on the. Sideways. When porters are moving a piece of furniture or a package they sometimes have to run it *on the sword* to be able to negotiate entry or exit.

T.

tabby. A very common but inexplicable simile is *as mad as a tabby*.

tail-tree. The long massive beam attached to the round-house of the old windmill to counterbalance the action of the points or sails when in motion. The tail-tree acted as a sort of rudder, and was used to bring the sails into, or to take them out of, the wind. It was anchored to the ground by means of strong ropes or chains.

take. When the tourist equipped with his attendant paraphernalia is addressed by some small boy with the words *Take me*, he need not fear that he is being requested to assume any other responsibility than to take his photograph.

take back. Sometimes used in the sense of 'overtake' as, *I can take he back in any bicycle race.*

take in. To be taken ill suddenly, as, *She took in the Sunday night, and they carried her to the hospital next day.*

tall-up. Very tall, as, *He was a big, tall-up man.*

tantalise. A very commonly used word, often with its correct meaning, but sometimes in sense of provoking to anger, as, *Child don't tantalise me!*

tar. (Slang.) Intoxicating liquor as, *Don't mind him: he got in his tar.* Hence **tarred,** intoxicated. The facetious term, **slap** tar, may also be noted: to walk some distance, not by inclination, but by force of circumstances.

tarass, trass. "Now rare or obsolete, 1612 ... To cover, coat, or lay with plaster", S.O.E.D. Tarass **mortar** is lime mortar with a small percentage of cement.

tarry. "Now literary" states the C.O.D., but still in colloquial use locally. *I trust there will be no long tarrying nôw*, a mason once said to me when I asked him when the job would be finished.

tayche. Thus the local spelling. The S.O.E.D. gives "Tache. 1657. (app. a. obs. or dial. F. tache, plate of iron.) *Sugar-boiling*. Each pan of the series through which the juice of the sugar-cane is passed in evaporating it, esp. the smallest and last of these, the *striking-t.*" Webster's *New International* lists it as "teache. (Also *tach, tache,* fr. Sp. *tacho, tacha.*) *Sugar Mfg,* Any, esp. the last of the series of

boilers or evaporating pans." With the new process of sugar manufacture, the tayche, tach, tache, teache is now a thing of the past.

tea. Used to refer to any warm drink, as sugar-tea, lime-tea, bush-tea,
and even cocoa-tea.

tea-meeting. The S.O.E.D. defines this function as a "public social
meeting (used in connection with a religious organisation) at which it
is taken"; but the local tea-meeting, which seems to have disappeared
from the scene shortly after the conclusion of the first world war,
requires, I think, a special note. It was a sort of prolonged concert
whose main features were songs, both solo and choral, and abundance
of refreshments, and a type of oratory that delighted in the display of
resounding polysyllabic words (some of them specially coined for the
occasion) and elaborate alliterative allusions to the great names of
history and literature. Preparations for the tea-meeting were begun
several months before the event, and admission was by ticket: one
shilling. The tea-meeting, usually held in a school hall or in the lodge
of a friendly society, adorned with evergreen branches and flowers,
began at nine o'clock with an oration by the vice-chairman, although
for an hour previously the choir-master and his carefully rehearsed
choir would have been welcoming the in-coming audience with a
selection from their repertoire. The vice-chairman would then address
the gathering reminding them that he was no great orator "such as
Plato or Dido, Demosthenes or Socrates", but only the forerunner of
the "man of gladness" who was now to entertain them. Amid great
cheering the chairman would then take his seat and the vice would
introduce him, exhorting him as being "fundamental and
groundamental enough to take and hold his place like Mark Antony or
Cicero, or Blake or Drake, or Wordsworth or Tennyson", etc ., etc.
"Take it and hold it," he would conclude "until the cock says *Claro
Clarum* pronouncing or announcing the break of day." The chairman
would then address the audience at some length after which the vice
would introduce to the chairman those who would provide the various
items of the programme. There would be solos, choruses, monologues,
dialogues, and "trialogues". The chairman would comment on each
item until the stroke of midnight, when there would be an intermission
of two hours for refreshment: large quantities of bread, biscuits,
sponge cakes and puddings, with large pots of boiling hot tea and
chocolate. Afterwards the songs and speeches would be resumed and

continue until daybreak.

teach. In warehouses where heavy bags of sugar, flour, etc., have to be shifted from place to place, the operation is performed by three or four pairs of men, each pair grasping the bag at opposite ends and passing to the next pair, and so on. This is known as teaching.

tell. Frequently used instead of the word, say, in such expressions as *Tell him goodbye,* or *Tell him howd'ye for me.*

tennis-ball. A small, round loaf of sweet bread.

thank-you-ma'am. See **swale.**

thick-copper. Old fashioned name for the penny to distinguish it from the **odd cent.**

thief. (Verb.) *He t'ief a foul from me once.* So, **t'iefin'** is preferred to thieving.

thing. The expression "thing" is often used instead of "and so forth", as, *He had plenty of cattle and sheep and thing.*

thingamerry, thingumbobsy. Cf. thingum, thingumajig, thingum bob, thingummy-bob, thingummy. S.O.E.D.

third gang. A term used to refer to the group of young labourers (aged 14 to 16) employed to do light tasks, like weeding, etc., on the sugar estate.

thrallia. Usually a small silver coin; also anything small and of no consequence, *I wouldn't give a thrallia for it.*

throw up. To pitch in, to pay a subscription to, as *Lewwe all throw up and buy a new ball.* Bruce Hamilton in his *Cricket in Barbados* notes one of the rules of the Carrington Cricking (sic) Club (1898): "I do hereby consider that all members must throw up a weekly subscription of 2 cents."

tie-tongue(d). Applied to one who speaks with a lisp or suffers from some impediment of his speech.

till-bury. A handy compound verb used on plantations signifying the process whereby a labourer at one and the same time tills the soil and buries or covers over such grass or weeds as might have been on the surface.

tiltman. A man on stilts. The tiltman was a popular figure on bank holidays.

timird. The intrusion of the letter "r", harking back to its Latin derivation is interesting; perhaps through confusion with "timorous",, a word which our eighteenth century forbears would no doubt have used.

tinnin. Most likely tinnen (adjective), cognate with wooden, brazen, etc., but used as a noun in place of tin, as, *The paling patch up with tinnin.* Also a tinnin is a large tin container, as, *Put the hog-food in the tinnin.*

tip. A small portion. Please for a tip of butter.

tisic. (Pronounced tizzick.) "Obsolete and dialectical form of phthsic" states the S.O.E.D. Only cats suffer from "the tisic" nowadays.

to-do-ment. To-do.

token. "A sign or presage of something to come, an omen, portent, or prodigy" (S.O.E.D.) is now obsolete in Standard English. *And when I saw all those beetles, I knew it was a token. I heard of my sister's death the next day.*

tom. A cheap cheerot. Also **long tom.**

too. Such exclamatory sentences as *You too love peas and rice!* or *You too like to be late for work!* with emphasis placed on the word, too, are much more common than "How you like peas and rice! ", etc.

took. (Noun.) Crude musical sounds: *to play took and banjo.*

toonkins, toonkuns. (Nursery) Term of endearment used to a child.

topsy. (Nursery). A chamber pot.

toreckly. It is quite impossible of course to list all the many and various words that are mispronounced, but some of them, for one reason or other, are so generally employed as to have almost acquired an identity of their own. Such a one is toreckly (directly), which is always used in the sense of immediately, or at most, in a very short time. *I'll fix this for you toreckly,* says the carpenter, and means it — at the time.

tot. "A very small drinking vessel; a child's mug. Chiefly dialect 1828", states the S.O.E.D. The Barbadian tot is a mug made of tin. The capacity of the tot varies; some tots may hold as much as a pint. "A tot of rum" thus conveys quite a different connotation to the Barbadian.

touchbam. A sort of miniature cannon, popular with the more venturesome and ingenious of small boys a few decades ago.

touchous. Touchy. Also U.S. dialect.

tow. In addition to its usual meaning, to give someone a ride on the cross-bar of a bicycle.

tra-la-la. Old-fashioned two-wheeled gig.

tradesman. Not one who is engaged in trade (grocer, butcher, etc.), but one who pursues some particular trade, as, shoemaker, tailor, etc.

trash. "Dried leaves of the sugar cane. Used as manure and also scattered on soil when young canes are growing to keep ground cool and to conserve moisture." *Harrisonian, July 1926.* Trash-**bone** the central rib of a dried cane leaf; trash-**heap** a large stack of trash.

traveller. (Slang.) A **snowball**. Snowballs are sold by vendors who push their carts around the district. The snowball is purchased and eaten *en route,* so to speak.

travers. Board planed crosswise to avoid ripping.

trildren. For some obscure reason this word is frequently used in preference to the more usual "children".

trouble. Used sometimes in the sense of interfere with or disturb, as, *Don't trouble my papers.* Two local proverbs: *Never trouble trouble till trouble trouble you,* and, *Trouble-tree don't bear no blossom.* Also the ejaculation, *Look a(t) trouble!,* on receipt of bad or disquieting news. J. Graham Cruikshank quotes a paralled instance from *Jeremiah*: *We looked for peace, but no good came: and for a time of health, and behold trouble.*

true. *He done it for true?* Has he really done it?

trust. Properly "To give a (person) credit for goods supplied; to supply with goods on credit" (S.O.E.D.) is most often used in the sense of obtaining such goods on trust, as, *I going trust a bread and some sugar from Miss Brathwaite shop.*

tuppence. $2^1/_2$ cents. See **fisherman's penny.**

turn. The phrase to *take a turn in someone,* i.e., to treat someone very roughly, may be noted. To turn **out**, of a boil, wound, etc., to become septic. Turn-**out** (noun), a funeral. See also **meeting.**

turn-over. A sort of sweet roll filled with coconut.

turn round. *After he was so nice to us he then turn round and cursed us.* Contradictory action or statement is implied by the use of this phrase.

tush-teeth. Projecting teeth.

twee nor twoh. If something is neither twee nor twoh, it is neither one thing nor yet another; it is just plain nonsense.

twin is usually regarded as dual noun, like pair, and a twin is consequently referred to as *one of a twin.*

two by four. Facetious term for a smallish house.

111

U.

ugly. (Noun). That which is normally or ethically discreditable, as, *God don't like ugly* (local proverb).

um. Although sometimes used with reference to some specific object, as, *Um is mine,* yet most often as the formal subject of the verb to be, as, *Um is a pity you don't mind your own business, Um ain't true.* etc.

un-. This prefix is usually pronounced "awn", as, awnderstand, awnhappy, etc. The word, "underneath", which is preferred to "under", has been metamorphosed into "awneat", as, *He was standing awneat a big umbrella.*

underlook. To look askance.

unfair. (Verb.) To treat unfairly. *He would have done better, but the master unfair him.*

unna. (Personal pronoun, probably of African origin.) This unusual word, together with its alternative form, **wunna,** is used to mean *all of you,* as, *Unna ain't got no manners?* or, *I got something to tell wunna.* Also unna **all** or wunna **all.**

up. (i) Frequently used redundantly with verbs of motion, or else to denote location, as, *When you coming up to see us?* or, *You live up by him?* (ii) The use of this word to express a complete or effectual result is of course Standard English idiom; such phrases as eat up, dry up, tear up, etc., etc., are of long established usage, and such innovations from U.S. as beat up and shoot up are now common currency, but the following local examples may strike oddly on English ears: crease up, dirty up, hug up, kiss up, wet up, ink up, play up (*Don't play up in the mud, child*), sweat up, wet up, etc., etc. Again, there are some others with specific meaning, noted elsewhere in this collection: **cock** up, **horse** up, **jump** up, **lick** up, **mash** up, **set** up, **skin** up, **work** up.

upperside. Generally speaking to the windward, or east. See also **lowside,** or **lowerside.**

upright. In expressions such as *upright six, upright twelve,* the word refers to the minute-hand of the clock, and thus signifies that it is exactly six o'clock, or exactly twelve o'clock.

upsided-down is for some quaint reason preferred to upside-down.

upstairs. (Adjective.) A two-storeyed house is always referred to as *an upstairs house.*

use. "To take or partake of as, food drink, etc., Now rare" states the S.O.E.D. But still very common locally, as, *You using the seaeggs for breakfast, mistress? You may not like sea-cats, but a lot o' people does use them.*

used. The second syllable is usually accented: u-zid.

V.

vap. (Slang.) To snap the fingers when throwing dice.

VERBAL MONGRELS. The conversion of two or more perfectly good English words into a slovenly compound with consequent distortion of its components is a practice certainly not to be encouraged: grammarians have deplored and etymologists ignored all such vulgar liberties being taken with the mother tongue. But the thing persists, and such horrors as meantersay, gorblimey, wonna, lemme, and leggo, for example have, by the insidious means of dialogue, now become part and parcel of our heritage of English literature. It is regrettable that Barbadians have, without the help of either Whitechapel or the Bowery, produced quite a formidable number of atrocities. Regrettable, but a fact nevertheless, and, as such, I have ventured to classify them under what I hope to be a sufficiently inelegant heading. For in daily use are to be heard in our midst the following: **blummah** (blow me) or its variant **gawblummah,** a milder form of the cockney oath; **cummah** (come here), as, *Cummah, girl, and tell me something;* **dahday** (that there), as, *What dahday is?* **hummuch** (how much), **summuch** (so much), and **tummuch** (too much), with of course their plurals **hummny, summny,** and **tummny; huckum** (how come why), although its use is regarded, I believe, as confined to the peasantry; the

113

plural of lemme, **lewwe** (let us), as, *Come lewwe fire one;* **lookah** (look here), as, *Lookah, man, who you think you is?* the almost un-recognizable **simmah** (see me), as, *Simma, boy!* an expression of delight which denotes that the speaker is doing something of which he is especially proud and is, by these words, drawing attention to himself and his performance; **tekkah** or **tekkay** (take care), as, *Tekka you mash me foot* and **wuffa** (what for) in the sense of Why should I?

vex. *I very vex with you.* I'm very angry with you.

VOWEL SOUNDS. As mentioned in the introduction of these *Notes* little attempt has been made to deal with the phonetics of Badian, but I think some reference should be made to certain vowel sounds. Broadly speaking there are few true vowel sounds: most of the vowels tend to be drawn out into diphthongs. Thus, the long vowel sounds, AH, AY, and O tend to become AH-UH, and O-UH, respectively. *Mah-un, for the go-aht.* The short vowel sounds AH and EH, as in *bag* and *leg,* are transformed into AH-EE and EH-EE respectively before G, as, *A bah-egg full of eh-eeggs.* After the sound, K, the vowel-sound AH becomes EE-AH, as *This mo-tor-cee-ahr cee-ahnt* (can't), *cee-ahrry so many people.* The diphthong, I, is pronounced like the Irish I, and this is unique in the West Indies. And special attention must be drawn to the sound UH, most nearly approximating to the short-vowel sounds: *Give it tuh muh* (to me); *That will do fuh yuh* (for you).

W.

wae. (Pronounced wah-ye.) Exclamation of pain.

wait. Barbadians seldom wait for a person, they wait on him as, *I've been waiting on you for the last half-hour.* Perhaps a survival of the courtly "waiting on someone's pleasure".

waiter. Still in general use to mean a tray or salver. Cf. dumb waiter.

Walker's. To be employed at *Walker's* (the name of a plantation) is a euphemism signifying that the person referred to is walking around seeking employment.

want. *The telephone wants yóu* is Standard Badian for "You are wanted at the telephone".

wares. The plural is preferred in referring to kitchen ware.

warri. A game which was brought from Africa during the days of slavery ("Warri; One of a tribe of Niger Delta speaking a dialect of the Beni language. *Webster's New International Dictionary*) and which is still very popular, both in Barbados and in West Africa. It is played on a rectangular board with six pairs of bowl-like depressions placed side by side. The smooth roundish seeds of the **horse-nicker** are used as counters.

was. Frequently inserted after 'had' to denote obligation, as, *It was raining so hard, I had was to shelter in the shop.*

wash. Used as a collective noun to denote a great number, as, a wash of people, cars, etc.

washer. Washerwoman, laundress.

watch. Used reflexively; be careful, look out. If you're about to try slipping through a traffic jam, you may hear a policeman call *Watch yourself.*

water-wash. (Verb). To rough-dry.

water-whelps. Dumplings made with little or no milk, water being used instead.

waxcat. An echo word much in vogue with players of dominoes when slamming the tiles on the board.

waxing kernel. A kernel, ("now dialect", S.O.E.D.) is sometimes called a waxing (or is it a waxen?) kernel.

way. The statement *I know that way* is often made instead of "I understand" or "I know what you mean"; e.g. as a response to the warning "Be careful with that parcel: it contains glassware," is given *Yes, I know that way.*

weather. Frequently used to mean bad weather. *Looks like we're in for some weather.* In a recent cricket broadcast one of the commentators announced before the start of the game: *It's a beautiful day here at Kensington; blue skies, gentle breeze, warm sun — no sign whatever of weather.*

wed. Commonly used as the past tense of weed.

weed. (slang.) An expert, as, *He's a weed, at it,* i.e. cricket, tennis, philandering, etc.

wee-wee. (Adjective.) Tiny, wee (see **COMPOUND REDUNDANT**). (Verb.) Urinate.

well. Frequently used instead of the adverb of degree, very, as, *It's well hot to-day.* Also to be noted in the use of **very** well, considerably, as, *He was sick for a few weeks very well,* i.e., for a considerable number of weeks; *I saw some people there very well* i.e., quite a few people. Very well is sometimes used instead of Thank you. Sometimes used when referring to the pit of a latrine.

well head. A very common phrase is to be *living at the well head,* i.e. to be living in very affluent circumstances, at the well's head.

wet. (Cricket.) *Wet him! Wet him!* is in an exhortation to a batsman to hit out at the bowling.

w'happenin'? i.e. What happening? is a familiar form of greeting instead of such salutations as *How goes it?* or *What's the news?*

what's fat? This once familiar street cry is no longer heard. It was the call of the **speculator** who, armed with a length of rope, was making his rounds on the lookout for a likely bargain.

whem. A wen.

which. Still used especially in parenthetical clauses, to refer to persons, as *Mr. Jones, which, as you may remember, was in charge of the goods.* Which **part**, or which **place**: where, as *Which part you get hurt? Which place you see him?*

whichin. Emphatic form of the relative, which, as, *He told me to go whichin I did.*

whistling frog. "The little leptodactylic toad, bearing the tongue-twisting name of Eleutherodactylus (formerly Hylodes) martinicensis, (Tschudi) ..." states Iris Bayley in *The Whistling Frogs of Barbados, B.H.M.S., Vol. XVII, No. 4,* an article which deals comprehensively with the ubiquitous little tree-frog.

whit-hole, pool. See **hole.**

white missy. A glass of white rum, a cheaper type of rum to which the colouring matter has not been added.

white rain. Rain from thin stratiform cloud as contrasted with showers from dark or heavy convective cloud.

whitleather. Not listed in C.O.D., but in the S.O.E.D. as "the tough ligament in the neck of an ox or other grazing animal, also called *paxwax* 1713". A tough piece of meat is said to be "like whitleather".

wh'side. Which side (place, district); as, *Wh'side you come from?*

windball. A tennis ball. Also 'hopping ball'.

wish. Often used instead of want, as, *Do you wish me?* Also used of inanimate things, as *The grass wish cutting too bad.*

wizzy-wizzy. Whispering, *Come on, speak out: no wizzy-wizzy-ing.*

woman cow. A freemartin. "Hermaphrodite or imperfect female of ox kind." C.O.D.

woman's tongue. See **shak-shak.**

wood ant. Termite.

wooden horses. Merry-go-round.

wood-slave. Gecko or white lizard. Also **poison** lizard.

words from the Windward parishes. The chrysalis of a moth is known as a *jack merino;* the ground dove as a *commienickie;* and the slug as *land beef.* A poor white or 'red leg' is also known as a *fotham.*

work. To affect the bowels, as by medicine or some other cause, as, *That stale fish work me all night.* Work **up:** (i) to till the soil (ii), to dance in a salacious manner.

worker. Pronounced in the Badian manner (see **PRONUNCIATION**), a dressmaker, seamstress. Possibly, originally, needleworker.

worm. A pimple. Many adolescents suffer from worms on the face. Cf. Mercutio's speech in *Romeo and Juliet*, Act. I, sc. 4:

> a small grey-coated gnat
> Not half so big as a little worm
> Pricked from the lazy finger of a maid.

writing-hand. For some reason this inversion is preferred to hand-writing.

wullay. Expression denoting despondency, sadness, grief, etc., as, *Wullay, wullay, what I going do now Mammy dead?* J. Graham Cruickshank in his *Black Talk (Argosy Co., Ltd., Demerara, 1916)* suggests its affinity with the "weylawey" of Chaucer, and the "waly, waly" of Ramsay.

wulloss. A possible variant of **wullay**; used much more frequently, most often to express disappointment or disgust, as, *Wulloss look what you gone and done now!*

wunna. See **unna.**

wussless, wutless. Variants of worthless, but implying a degree of depravity not necessarily associated with the word. Wussless may also be used as a substantive, in which case it is merely a playful form of address, as, *Hello, wussless, how things going?*

Y.

yacht-boat. (see **COMPOUND REDUNDANT.**)

yam. (Slang.) To eat ravenously or greedily, as, *Don't yam it like that, boy.* African *nyam:* eat.

yard-boy. A boy employed to do odd jobs out-of-doors.

yard fowl. A characterless, weakly acquiescent person; a yes-man. Political term of abuse.

yellow-bird. *"Dendroica capitalis Lawr* ... a small bird of a conspicuous bright yellow colour, duller on the back, wings, and tail, and with streaks of brown on the throat ... a member of the very large family of the New World Warblers, found all over America and the West Indies." Mrs. P.C. K. Anderson *Some Observations on the Birds of Barbados, B.M.H.S.*

yellow-breast. The **sugar-bird.**

your all's. This quaint possessive of the popular you all is extremely common. *I had no idea this house was your all's.*

yuh. Tacked on at the end of a sentence, this sound expresses a warning, even a threat, as, *Don't do that, yuh!*

yumma. Pus. Really, humour. The local pronunciation of the word will be better excused when it is remembered that "the pronunciation of the initial *h* is only recent", S.O.E.D. It is quite possible that the local use of the word is in accordance with its original meaning, "Any fluid or juice of an animal, or plant either natural or morbid", S.O.E.D. Cf. aqueous humour and vitreous humour of the eye.

ADDENDA

BROADCASTITIS. There has been a tendency of late among an increasing number of announcers to accentuate the former syllable of many dissyllabic words whose latter syllable should be stressed. These distortions are far too numerous to list; I shall give as examples just a few that have assailed my ears during the past week: COM/plete, CON/cern, DIS/pute, EX/am, RE/sult, SUC/cess, and believe it or not, POL/ice. But the most shattering of these travesties is made of the word 'event', whose modest short initial vowel is stressed and lengthened to such an extent, that hardly a

119

day passes without reference to some EE/*vent.* One can only hope that our everyday speech will not be AD/versely AF/fected by this verbal epidemic.

NEOLOGISMS. There are three words which I should like to include in this collection, but I doubt very much whether they have ever been part of our common speech. Indeed, as I have only heard them used by two persons, I am forced to conclude that they were happy inventions on their part. But the words are so richly evocative, that I hope I may be excused listing them. The first and third words form part of my earliest recollections, since they were used frequently by my nurse whose speech was both grammatical and devoid of malapropisms. The second word was used regularly by a well-educated woman, a friend of mine.

copygowchie. A quaint or comical drawing such as a child might make.

frazma. A confused or involved state of mind, but not so acute as to be termed a frenzy, of which no doubt it is a derivative.

shinnavericks. A term of endearment. *What has my little shinnavericks been doing this morning?*

VERBIAGE. I suppose we are all called upon at sometime or other to provide testimonials for various persons. The following recommendation, quite genuine, which was presented to me some years ago, attains such heights of sublime verbosity, that I hope it may relieve the monotony of perusing these Notes:

Having a right knowledge of his chart and compass of Life I therefore ascribe him as a chaste benevolent and profound Labourer from a loyal grade of sincere inability and honest conduct outwardly seen and manifested by His love and kind affectionate policy. No blackguard. Very pious and gentle towards all human grade sensible. Educated to a conspicuous demand against all other humane policies. His retrograde becomes Compliable with all other well known faculties as should be agreeable to all other corresponding views of servitude.

F.A.C.